Grand Tours of the World

LANDS
OF THE NILE

Grand Tours of the World

LANDS OF THE NILE

EAST AFRICA
ETHIOPIA
SUDAN
EGYPT

TORSTAR BOOKS
NEW YORK • TORONTO

ACKNOWLEDGMENTS

Grand Tours of the World
LANDS OF THE NILE

Published by
TORSTAR BOOKS INC.
41 Madison Avenue
Suite 2900
New York, N.Y. 10010

Original French edition *Beautés du Monde* produced by
LIBRAIRIE LAROUSSE
Editors: Suzanne Agnely, Jean Barraud, J. Bonhomme, N. Chassériau, L. Aubert-Audigier
Designers: A.-M. Moyse, N. Orlando, E. Riffe, H. Serres-Cousiné
Copy editors: L. Petithory, B. Dauphin, P. Artistide
Cartographer: D. Horvath

English edition edited & designed by
ST. REMY PRESS
Editor: Kenneth Winchester
Art director: Pierre Léveillé
Designers: Diane Denoncourt, Odette Sévigny
Picture researcher: Michelle Turbide
Contributing editors: Nancy Coté, David Dunbar

Printed in Belgium

Library of Congress Cataloging in Publication Data

ISBN 1-55001-050-6

In conjunction with **Grand Tours of the World**
Torstar Books offers a 12-inch raised relief world globe.
For more information write to:
Torstar Books Inc.
41 Madison Avenue
Suite 2900
New York, N.Y. 10010

CONTENTS

DISCOVERING THE NILE

At once the greatest and most mysterious river on earth, the Nile is the unifying thread of life stitching together a third of a continent, connecting the African and the Arab worlds, the past and the present. It rises deep in the heart of Africa, and flows north for 4,000 miles to the blue Mediterranean.

On its epic journey, the western branch of the river pours into Lake Victoria, the world's second-largest body of fresh water (after Lake Superior). It tumbles over Kabalega Falls, picks up the flow of streams issuing from lakes Edward and Albert, then eases into the vast and swampy Sudd, where it loses much of its water to evaporation. If finally emerges from that watery labyrinth as the White Nile, and parallels the Blue Nile for hundreds of miles in the Sudan before joining its sister stream at Khartoum.

This coupling of the Blue and White Nile is referred to in Arabic poetry as "the longest kiss in history." Farther north, the unified Nile tumbles over the six cataracts that hindered early exploration, then passes through Egypt, its valley a green serpentine refuge against the brown of the desert. It flows past the crumbling pillars of Abu Simbel and Karnak, monuments to the golden age of Egyptian civilization; past ancient Memphis and the pyramids of Giza; on through the heart of Cairo, capital of the Arab world; and finally out to the fertile fan of the Delta.

The source of Africa's river of legend eluded the pharaohs, baffled Greek and Roman explorers, and fascinated Victorian scientists. "Of the source of the Nile no one can give any account," wrote Herodotus, who only made it as far as the first cataract at Aswan before turning back in frustration about 460 B.C.

For more than 2,000 years, the source of the river remained a magnificent obsession for geographers. In 1858, John Hanning Speke reached Lake Victoria. On a subsequent expedition in 1862, the English explorer discovered a river flowing northward from the lake and cabled home that the mystery had been solved.

But the intrepid English explorers who followed in his wake—Richard Burton, David Livingstone, Henry Morton Stanley—proved that the true source of the Nile lay even farther south. Soon it was discovered that the Kagera River fed more water into Lake Victoria than any other—it could properly be called the true headwater. The Kagera was traced 500 miles southwest of its entrance into the lake to a hill in southern Burundi. There, in 1937, German explorer Dr. Burkhart Waldecker found a

tiny spring: the font of the Kagera and the beginning of the Nile. The spring is marked with a small pyramid bearing a weathered inscription on a metal plaque: *Caput Nili*—"Source of the Nile."

Any yet there is more. The spring is just the source of the Victoria Nile. The Albert Nile flows from the fabled Ruwenzori range—six snowcapped peaks straddling the Equator in northern Uganda. The Nile begins here as well, as ice. Ptolemy immortalized these peaks, which he called the Mountains of the Moon, and in an inspired bit of guesswork, listed them in A.D. 150 as the source of the Nile.

The Albert and Victoria Nile eventually form the White Nile. But what about the Blue Nile, which joins the White at Khartoum, contributing 20 percent of the Nile's single stream? Here, there is no confusion about the source—a reservoir in the Ethiopian highlands called Lake Tana. Soon after the Blue Nile exits the lake, it thunders over a falls the Ethiopians called "Great River Smoke," then rips through a spectacular mile-deep gorge that rivals the Grand Canyon.

In Egypt, the land most closely associated with the Nile, there are two distinct modern eras—before El Sadd el-Aali (the Aswan High Dam) and after. Through the

ages, Egyptians have deplored the caprice of the river. "If he is sluggish the nostrils are stopped up," complained one ancient text, "and all men are brought low. The offerings of the gods are diminished, and millions perish from among mankind."

But no more. The dream to regulate the Nile became a reality in 1971 with the completion of the Aswan High Dam, which contains enough stone to build 17 Great Pyramids. In fact, it is the greatest engineering feat since the pyramids at Giza were raised beside the river 45 centuries earlier. Ethiopia and other countries south of the dam have recently suffered through a terrible famine, but Egypt has been spared, freed at last from her neighbors' cycles of drought and despair.

But the Nile has found ways to take its revenge on those who harness it. The dam has worsened downstream erosion, increased soil salinity and destroyed the coastal sardine industry. In addition, about 100,000 Nubian villagers were forced to relocate from their flooded homeland, and priceless archeological treasures have disappeared forever. The river, harnessed but never tamed, still rules the destiny of Egypt.

EAST AFRICA

"The East" is a term laden with connotations of the exotic, the mysterious, the spiritual, as though the mere act of journeying eastward conferred these qualities on the landscape.

East Africa is not only "oriental" because of its geographical location, but also because it has long been influenced by peoples from across the Red Sea and the Indian Ocean. By the 11th century, Persians and Arabs had founded colonies on the coast of East Africa, and were carrying on active trade with nations as far off as Malaysia. By the 19th century, the "peculiar institution" of slavery was centered on the island of Zanzibar, as Arabs penetrated to the heart of Africa, plundering tribes for their wicked business.

"When the pipes are played on Zanzibar, all Africa east of the lakes must dance," the slavers used to boast.

The tune changed one night in 1964, when hundreds of Arabs died in an African uprising. The last Sultan of Zanzibar fled to England. And the new rulers—the Afro-Shirazi Party—agreed to merge Zanzibar with the newly independent Tanganyika to form the United Republic of Tanzania. Then all Africa east of the lakes danced—this time with joy.

This dark legacy is offset by a happier, and much older, heritage. Africa east of the lakes is considered one of the cradles of mankind, home of the earliest bipeds, who took the first tentative steps on the evolutionary road in the Great Rift Valley

that cuts through the heart of the region. At Lake Turkana in northern Kenya, on Rusinga Island in Lake Victoria, in the Olduvai Gorge of Tanzania and dozens of other sites, scientists have pieced together bone fragments, crude stone tools and fossils in an effort to trace the roots of man's family tree.

In Tanzania's remote central plateau region, prehistoric man left galleries of his art adorning cliff faces and rock outcroppings, a testament to the skill and creativity of untold generations of painters. No one knows who the artists were or even when they lived. The paintings could not have endured the elements for more than a few thousand years, but carbon-14 tests indicate the pigments are much older.

▲ *Kenya: Lake Nakuru National Park is best known for its huge colonies of flamingos, although hippos also find the waters to their liking.*

11

The pictures emphasize game, which suggests the Stone-Age tribe was comprised of hunter-gatherers, rather than pastoralists. (The only domestic animal depicted is a dog.) Drawings of hartebeests, giraffes, antelope, even an elephant hunt adorn the craggy canvas of the cliffs. Humans are shown as dancers, hunters and musicians with notes pouring from their instruments.

The present population of this region is remarkably diverse. There are 124 distinct tribes in Tanzania, 70 in Kenya and 36 in Uganda. Yet these often diverse groups come from only two main tribes — the Bantus and the Nilotics. The Bantus arrived first. Their forefathers were paleonegritic peoples, like the Bushmen and

Pygmies, who were driven south and east to this part of Africa.

No one is certain when the Nilotic herdsmen first penetrated this region, but they probably came from the north in successive waves from the fifth to the 15th centuries A.D. Relations with the Bantus varied from open hostility to uneasy coexistence. Even today, there is a certain distance between members of the two

▲ *Young Masai warriors, often distinguished by dung-and-mud headdresses, become* morans, *or warriors, as soon as they are circumcised.*

◄ *This young Masai woman wears necklaces of brightly colored glass beads which signify her status—and that of her husband.*

tribes, particularly in Kenya and Uganda. In Kenya, the rivalry between the Nilotic Luos and the Bantu Kikuyus is a major factor in political life.

The Kikuyus, one of East Africa's largest ethnic groups, claim the fertile foothills of Mount Kenya as their homeland. Land disputes between Kikuyu farmers and their British counterparts touched off the bloody Mau Mau move-

ment of the early 1950s. With Kenya's independence, many Kikuyu, including the nation's first chief of state, Jomo Kenyatta, rose to positions of power.

One of East Africa's most independent-minded tribes is the Masai, Nilotic herdsmen who live in the Great Rift Valley in Tanzania and Kenya. They refuse to cultivate the land and have little to do with other tribes. Small family groups

travel with the seasons, building clusters of elongated huts ringed with thorn fences. Their skill in cattle breeding has made the Masai among Africa's wealthiest pastoralists.

Another tribe that turns its back on the 20th century is the Turkana, who make their home by the lake of the same name in northern Kenya. They migrated some 200 years ago from Uganda and Ethiopia,

▲ *The squat huts of the Masai are made of cow dung spread over a frame of bound branches. Women act as architects and builders; the men hunt and tend the cattle.*

and now tap the lake's bounty. Huge Nile perch weighing 200 pounds or more lurk in Turkana's depths; the species survives from a time when the lake had a direct link with the Nile.

Many Turkana forego lakeside life and wander with their herds of cattle, camels, goats and sheep through the arid lands between Turkana and the Uganda border. Their ancient custom of cattle rustling has won them a well-deserved notoriety.

The Turkana reputation is known by a related tribe in northeast Uganda, the Karamojong, who have also been known to replenish herds ravaged by drought with the occasional raid. Karamojong cherish their cattle above all else. Livestock is rarely butchered, except on ceremonial occasions. Tribesmen give each member of their herd a name, train them to come when called, sing to them and of them. They even supplement their diets by mixing milk with protein-rich blood drawn from a cow's jugular vein.

Cattle also form the basis of social relationships. To win a wife, a groom

▲ *The twin peaks of Mount Kenya, Africa's second-highest summit (after Tanzania's Mount Kilimanjaro), rise 17,058 feet. At the dawn of time, says a Kikuyu legend, the Divider of the Universe created Mount Kenya as his home.*

14

▲ Kenya: Like creatures out of the mists of time, flamingos feed in brackish Lake Nakuru. For fresher drinking water, the birds fly north to the steaming springs of Lake Harrington.

gives each of his bride's relatives an animal. This gift earns him their lifelong support. If rich in cattle, a man may seek more than one spouse to fetch his water, till his fields and bear his children.

Adding to this complex mix of tribes is the Asian population. During the colonial era, eastern influence was perpetuated by Indians and Pakistanis, who poured into the region to help build the railroads. Many stayed on to work as merchants and civil servants, highly visible roles which fueled the resentment of the indigenous peoples. In 1972, dictator Idi Amin expelled 70,000 Asians, which pleased many Ugandans but crippled the country's economy. After Kenya's independence in 1963, thousands of Asians opted for British rather than Kenyan citizenship, then found themselves out of a job, victims of a long-range program of "Africanization."

Offsetting this multiplicity, though, is an unusual phenomenon in East Africa: the existence of a common language, Swahili. This lingua franca may contribute to a profound unity, more marked than in any other part of Africa. There is an East African "atmosphere," reflected in a contemplative temperament, more deeply attached to the permanence of things. In a word, more "oriental."

▲ *Kenya: Haloed in ostrich feathers, this artistically adorned young man is a member of the Kikuyu tribe, the country's largest ethnic group.*

▲ *Kenya: Related to the Masai, the Samburu are nomadic pastoralists who live mainly on milk and blood from their animals.*

Another common bond of these three countries is the region's greatest gift to the world: its incomparable wildlife. The great game areas lie close to the Great Rift Valley and its chain of lakes: Serengeti, Mara, Amboseli, Tsavo, Selous, and dozens of other parks, sanctuaries, conservation areas and forest reserves.

One of the most scenic spots in Africa is Tanzania's Ngorongoro Crater, em-

braced in a conservation unit. The crater is the world's largest intact caldera, the collapsed crater of an extinct volcano. It is large enough to hold the entire city of Paris. Within the 2,000-foot-high walls is a self-contained community of plains animals, including the rare black rhino and 11 prides of lions.

Another of nature's spectacular displays is presented by East Africa's flamingos, which thrive on the desolate alkaline lakes of the Great Rift Valley. Flamingos band together in huge flocks for safety and for the courtship displays necessary for breeding. Honking and jostling, displaying birds parade stiff-necked through a throng of neighbors. The dance continues intermittently for weeks.

The region has about three million lesser flamingos and more than 50,000 greater flamingos. When this colourful horde descends on Kenya's Lake Nakuru, it consumes up to 200 tons of food a day, mainly algae.

Here, nature seems almost ostentatious in its abundance, in terms of both sheer numbers of animals and variety of species. This wealth of wildlife has made East Africa the prime destination for nature lovers from all over the world.

▲ *Tanzania: The striated slopes of Ol Donyo Lengai are sacred to the Masai. This active volcano last erupted in 1966.*

Kenya:
A Pride of Wildlife

A pride of lions basking in the noonday sun, zebras galloping across the savanna, Masai warriors brandishing spears...to many people Kenya *is* Africa. The romance and excitement of wildlife safaris—with photographers, not hunters, doing most of the shooting—have turned Kenya into East Africa's most popular tourist destination.

Kenya is a geographically and culturally complex land. Larger than France and Belgium combined, the country consists of three major landscapes: the drowsy coastal lowlands where Arab slave traders founded settlements in the seventh century; the parched scrubland and searing desert of the north and east; and the western highlands flanking the lake-dotted Great Rift Valley.

The country's mix of more than 70 tribes, plus Arabs, Asians and Europeans (mainly British), matches the country's diverse landscapes. The coastal lowland is characterized by Arab and Malay influences, with Islam in ascendence. The lowland plains of the northeast are inhabited by Nilotic tribes closely related to the neighboring Somalis. East of the Great Rift Valley live the Bantu tribes—mainly

◀ *Faster than a lion, the cheetah is one of the deadliest denizens of the African grasslands.*

▲ *Tsavo National Park: On a solitary stroll to the old watering hole, this elephant owes its ruddy color to a mud bath—protection against insects. The Tsavo elephant herd is 10,000 strong, one of the continent's greatest concentrations.*

►*Amboseli National Park (overleaf): Its snowy crown thrust above the clouds, Mount Kilimanjaro in Tanzania provides a backdrop of incomparable beauty to this Kenyan park.*

19

the Kikuyu who form a sixth of Kenya's population of ten million. West of the valley, along the shores of Lake Victoria, Nilotic tribes predominate, especially the Luo. In the valley itself live the Masai.

The mile-high city of Nairobi, dubbed the "safari capital of the world," was founded only 80 years ago as a makeshift camp during the construction of the Kenya-Uganda Railroad. Today, with a fast-growing population of one million, it is one of Africa's largest and most beautiful cities. Blessed with a springlike climate most of the year, Nairobi has numerous parks and broad avenues lined with exotic trees and shrubs, thus earning its Masai name of Nakusontelon ("the beginning of all beauty").

Many of Nairobi's sights are within easy walking distance of the hotel district, which has some 8,000 beds, ranging from economy to deluxe international. As a primer on Kenya's natural history, the National Museum, with its collection of African butterflies (said to be the world's largest) is well worth a visit. There is also an exhibit of Joy Adamson's paintings of

▲ Mombassa: Filigreed sanctuary of faith, this Hindu temple is dedicated to the god Shiva. Asians were originally brought to Kenya by the British to build the Kenya-Uganda Railroad.

wildflowers and the people of Kenya, and a section displaying exciting recent prehistoric finds near Lake Turkana.

Nearby are the Nairobi Aviary, with a collection of African birds, and Snake Park, which contains Nile crocodiles, 200 species of snakes, and other kinds of reptiles. Visitors can watch poisonous snakes being milked for their venom, which is used in anti-venom serums.

Nairobi's most compelling site can be seen from the summit of the Ngong Hills, described in luminous prose by Danish-born author Karen Blixen in the 1937 masterpiece *Out of Africa*. In one direction is the 20th-century capital; in the other, the primeval African grasslands of Nairobi National Park, bordered on the west and northeast by Nairobi suburbs, but open to the migrations of game from the Athi Plains to the south.

The park was established as the country's first sanctuary in 1947 to protect wildlife being slaughtered by troops garrisoned in Nairobi during the Second World War. Here, just five miles from downtown, bushbuck and impala roam hardwood forests, and lions and cheetahs share the open plain with gazelles, zebras and wildebeests.

Kenya's varied terrain and population (80 percent of the people live in only 15 percent of the land area, mostly in the Lake Victoria basin and highlands) make the country an ideal wildlife habitat. Kenya has responded by developing one of the world's most extensive park systems, with nearly 40 parks and game reserves accounting for six percent of the country's land area.

About two dozen parks are accessible to the average tourist. Many consider the Masai Mara Game Reserve, 155 miles west of Nairobi, the best of Kenya's wildlife sanctuaries, where animals that roam the plains—and their predators—can still be found in great numbers.

The "Mara," as it is known, is an extension of Tanzania's great Serengeti National Park, a juxtaposition that permits one of the continent's great wildlife spectacles. Around July, hundreds of thousands of zebras and wildebeests from the Serengeti thunder across the border to feed on the lush savanna of Kenya.

These rolling grasslands, veined with green acacia woodlands along the Mara and Talek rivers, are also home to buffalo, gazelles and topi. Thornbush thickets shelter black rhinos, elephants and tall giraffes. Not surprisingly, with all this food wandering about, the park is re-

nowned for its predators. Lions, in particular, can often be seen roaming the plains in prides of 20 or 30.

Here, the Masai are allowed to graze their cattle, which provide the tribe with a food supply of blood, milk and meat. The origins of the Masai have long puzzled anthropologists; one turn-of-the-century theory identified them as one of the lost tribes of Israel. Later studies did

find Semitic and Babylonian traces in the Masai, who built a 17th-century empire that extended from Mount Kenya to southern Tanzania.

The vast preserve of Tsavo National Park, which covers 8,000 square miles, embraces volcanic cones, bushland and high escarpments. Most visitors are drawn to Mzima Springs, where luxuriant vegetation surrounds large pools of clear water, home to hippos and crocodiles. The grasslands thunder with the park's 10,000 resident elephants.

Just 50 miles from Tsavo's eastern border lies the humid Kenyan coast, a world apart that seems to belong more to the Middle East than sub-Saharan Africa. Arab traders breezed in on monsoon winds and founded settlements along this tropical shore from the first century B.C.

onward. Today, the Old Town of Mombassa, Kenya's second-largest city, retains its Arab flavor. A maze of narrow streets twists past houses with overhanging balconies and intricately carved doorways. Goldsmiths and silversmiths practice their crafts; traders peddle carpets, brassware and aromatic spices. South of town, the beach is shaded with pendanus palms and wispy casuarina.

▲ *Broad beaches of fine white sand back much of Kenya's coastline. Superb fishing, extensive offshore coral reefs and a well-developed complex of resort hotels have made this area an ocean playground.*

Uganda: Pearl of Africa

Uganda contains some of the finest landscapes in Africa: the green and mountainous southwest, a region of clear lakes and wooded hills; the towering Ruwenzori Mountains along the western border, cloaked in tropical forest; the grasslands of the northeast, home to ostriches, hartebeests and gazelles; and, forming the southern boundary, the vast expanse of Lake Victoria.

Few African countries are so well-watered as Uganda. This abundance of lakes, rivers, streams and dependable rainfall makes survival easier for the country's 12 million inhabitants, whose staple diet includes green bananas (*matoke*), cassava and sweet potatoes. The

▲ *Uganda: At Kabalega Falls (formerly Murchison Falls), the Nile plunges 140 feet, thunders through a 20-foot-wide bottleneck and spills into Lake Albert before continuing its 2,800-mile journey to the Mediterranean.*

▲ *Uganda: Few African countries are so well-watered as Uganda, a bounty that combines with rich soil and a temperate climate to support a diversity of crops, from bananas to cotton, tea to cassava.*

nile teems with fish, banana plantations dot the southern foothills, and large herds of cattle are grazed on the wide savannah.

One European visitor overwhelmed by this verdant land was the young Winston Churchill, who called Uganda the "pearl of Africa." Churchill claimed, "Uganda is a fairy tale. You climb up a railway instead of a beanstalk, and at the top there is a wonderful new world."

Unfortunately, Uganda has been plagued by tribal differences since its independence from Britain in 1962. Dictator Idi Amin seized power in 1971 and brutalized the country for seven bloody years before being toppled in a military coup organized by troops from Tanzania and ragtag Ugandan exiles. Four successive governments have failed to halt the anarchy, murder and chaos that torment this beautiful but battered land.

Before 1972, Uganda was all but self-sufficient in agriculture; under Amin, the people reverted to subsistence farming. Uganda's tourist industry also collapsed with the Amin regime. Today, travel is still difficult, with decaying roads and the occasional maurauding bands of thieves. This lamentable situation deprives Uganda's three great national parks— Ruwenzori, Kabalega and Kidepo Valley—of the international attention they so richly deserve.

Kidepo Valley, along the northern border with Sudan, contains broad savanna studded by flat-topped acacia trees. This is the haunt of elephants and zebras, and such rare species as the greater kudu, Bright's gazelle and Chandler's reed buck.

Kabalega Falls National Park to the southwest shelters one of Uganda's scenic wonders, a cataract on the Victoria Nile. As the river approaches the 140-foot drop formerly known as Murchison Falls, its bed narrows until the compressed torrent roars through a 20-foot channel in a fury of foaming water and mist.

The teeming wildlife of Ruwenzori National Park, bounded by lakes George and Edward, rivals the looming volcanic peaks for scenic supremacy. Lions, hippos, elephants, Uganda kob, warthogs and chimpanzees are just a few names on the wildlife roll call.

Looming above all are the Ruwenzori peaks, with mounts Stanley, Speke and Baker all over 15,000 feet. The lower slopes of these eerie summits are drenched with more than 200 inches of rain a year (Ruwenzori means "rainmaker" in a local dialect). At the 12,000-

foot level, plants reach bizarre sizes and forms: 40-foot-high groundsels; tree lobelia which tower over the heads of hikers; and multicolored moss carpeting the forest floor to a depth of several feet— the spongy home of earthworms that grow to three feet in length.

Around A.D. 150, Ptolemy hypothesized that the Nile was born in the runoff from the Ruwenzori, which he dubbed the Mountains of the Moon. The astronomer from Alexandria wasn't too far off; the southernmost branch of the Nile rises in the mountains of Rwanda and Burundi, a short distance south.

In Uganda, there is no single Nile. Rather, the river is a network of streams, rivers and lakes that join to create what is called the Albert Nile. Lake Victoria, fed by dozens of rivers, gives birth to the Victoria Nile, which flows north into Lake Kyoga, exits to the west, tumbles over Kabalega Falls, and flows into the northern end of Lake Albert. Lake Albert is fed in the south by the Semliki River, which drains lakes Edward and George, which are in turn fed by rivers that rise in the Ruwenzori. From Lake Albert, the Albert Nile emerges as a single stream.

Kampala is built, like Rome, on seven hills, each dominated by a particular feature. Among the more prominent

summit structures in Uganda's capital are the Anglican and Roman Catholic cathedrals and a mosque. On Mengo Hill stands the Twekobe royal palace, where the kings of Buganda held court. This dynasty lasted from the 1300s until 1966, when Prime Minister Milton Obote deposed King Freddie—King Edward Frederick Mutesa II. Obote's commander was a young colonel named Idi Amin.

▲ *Tanzania: Just 200 miles south of the equator, Mount Kilimanjaro thrusts its glacier-clad summit more than 17,000 feet above the plain.*

Kasubi Hill is the site of the Kabaka's Tombs ("kabaka" means king), the resting place of King Freddie. The tombs, which are open to the public, represent some of the country's finest thatched buildings.

Kampala straddles the equator, yet its setting in the cool uplands makes for a comfortable climate. Tree-lined avenues brightened with flowerbeds and shaded with palms wind along valleys and up the hills. Entebbe, a short distance south on the shore of Lake Victoria, is the site of botanical gardens with a fine collection of Africa's tropical trees and plants.

East of Entebbe, the lake's slate waters flow through a narrow rock gap and rush northward as the Victoria Nile. Until 1937, when the river's origins were discovered in Burundi, this was considered the headwaters of the great river.

Near its outlet from the lake, the Victoria Nile has been harnessed at the Owens Falls Dam. Electricity generated by ten turbines satisfies almost all of Uganda's power needs and 40 percent of Kenya's as well. In the midst of this development, a bit of ancient Africa endures at a golf course near the power station. The house rules permit players to move a ball stuck in hippo tracks.

▲ *Ngorongoro Crater: Part of a 3,200-square-mile conservation area, this caldera drops 2,000 feet below the plains, forming a special world where a rich diversity of wildlife thrives.*

Tanzania: Cradle of Mankind

East Africa's largest country stretches from humid tropical lowlands by the Indian Ocean to the shores of Africa's three largest lakes, Nyasa in the south, Tanganyika in the west, and Victoria in the north. Between the lakes and the lowlands stretches the semiarid Masai Steppe, which comprises more than half of the country. Conservation-minded Tanzanians have set aside almost a quarter of their land, much of it in the steppe, as game reserves, conservation areas, forest preserves and national parks to protect the nation's greatest resource, its magnificent wildlife.

In Tanzania, the Great Rift Valley splits into two arms. The eastern arm angles northeast through the heart of the country. The western arm wanders northwest to the border with Zaire, Burundi, Rwanda and Uganda.

Volcanic activity in the eastern section of the rift has thrust the cone of Kilimanjaro abruptly above the rolling grasslands near the Kenyan border. The glaciered summit of the 19,340-foot mountain is visible from a hundred miles in any direction. Kibo Peak, the most recent eruption site in the still-smoldering volcano, bears three concentric craters.

Another volcanic wonder in the rift is the Ngorongoro Crater, an enormous caldera that measures about 10 miles by 12 miles and drops 2,000 feet below the rim. Once a mountain, Ngorongoro collapsed in on itself when molten material underlying the cone was spewed out, leaving an empty chamber and a weakened foundation that could not support the weight of the rock above.

The floor of the crater is carpeted with grass and dotted with stands of trees. Many of East Africa's four million flamingos feed on the algae-rich waters of a shallow lake here. The crater also shelters thousands of wildebeests, zebras, antelopes, baboons and predators such as cheetahs, lions, jackals and hyenas.

Northwest of Ngorongoro is Africa's most celebrated treasure-house of wildlife, Serengeti National Park. Established some 60 years ago, it now shelters the greatest concentration of large mammals on earth. The annual migration in

May or June of 500,000 wildebeests from the central plains en route to permanent waterholes in Kenya is one of nature's great spectacles.

Just outside the park boundaries is the Olduvai Gorge, one of the cradles of mankind. Beginning in 1959, when the Leakeys unearthed a skull 1.8 million years old, the 25-mile-long gorge has yielded a wealth of early human remains.

▲ *Zanzibar: A former sultanate, this tropical island joined with the mainland in 1964.*

Three hundred feet deep, Olduvai's well-exposed strata offer a clear record of the past. Later Stone Age hunters lived in the highlands south of Olduvai, leaving in Kondoa district a legacy of more than 1,000 vivid rock paintings depicting human and animal life.

Today Tanzania is home to 14 million people, representing more than 100 tribes, united under President Nyerere's brand of socialist, non-aligned self-reliance. The capital of the United Republic, which includes the storied island of Zanzibar, is Dar es Salaam, which means "Haven of Peace." The city has few attractions, but it does possess a beautiful harbor.

A 20-minute flight from Dar es Salaam brings travelers to Zanzibar, one of the world's most beautiful islands. Sapphire waters sheltered by offshore reefs wash beaches of pure white sand. Feathery coconut palms tower above the lush foliage, and the smell of cloves wafts over the buildings of the old Arab quarter. Zanzibar once supplied four-fifths of the world's cloves (the spice supplanted slaves as the island's main industry), but declining prices and neglected plantations have reduced the harvest to a fraction of its former bounty.

▲ *Serengeti National Park: Lords of all they survey, these lions no longer follow the enormous herds of wildebeests on their migrations through the park. Instead they stay put in the center of the Serengeti and let their food come to them.*

ETHIOPIA

Ethiopia is an African anomaly. This country on the Horn of Africa, nearly three times the size of California, was never colonized by a European power. In fact, Ethiopia itself was expansionist. Beginning about the first century A.D., the Kingdom of Askum (and later the Christian Amharan empire) spread out from the highlands in the center of the country, seizing territory and conquering peoples.

As the empire evolved, the Amhara people came to dominate the feudal society, claiming most of the land and confiscating half of all crops, as well as charging a labor service from subjugated peoples. These imperialist policies, which continued well into the 19th century, have returned to haunt this ancient land, which now embraces about 31 million people, some 80 ethnic groups, and almost as many languages.

Today Africa's oldest independent country is an embattled realm. In 1974, after years of unrest over Haile Selassie's feudal rule, a group of junior officers imprisoned their commanders and seized power. The group deposed the emperor, ending a 2,000-year-old line of succession, (the aging monarch died in detention in 1975), and pronounced Ethiopia Marxist-Leninist.

A decade of drought has ravaged the provinces of Welo and Tigre, killing at least 200,000 people, and turning once-productive land into desert. Relief efforts were thwarted by two regional wars that have plagued the country for decades.

Along the coast of the Red Sea, Eritrea Province, once an autonomous region until annexed by Haile Selassie, has been fighting for independence since 1961 — Africa's longest armed conflict. Nomads in Ogaden Province have been battling the central government in bitter guerilla skirmishes since 1977. More than a million refugees from the conflict have given Somalia the greatest refugee problem in the world.

Despite its grave troubles, Ethiopia boasts landscapes of stunning beauty and diversity. The heart of Ethiopia is a vast central plateau rising 7,000 to 10,000 feet above the surrounding sun-seared plains and deserts. The country's best land and most temperate climate are found on the plateau, a kind of huge rock fortress.

▲ *Well-suited to the hot, dry climate, the hump-backed zebu is the most common cattle breed in Ethiopia.*

This tabletop is far from smooth. River gorges slash its volcanic rock, rounded hills rumple the land north of the capital of Addis Ababa, and mountains jutting high above the plateau have been eroded into the characteristic mesa-like *ambas* of the Ethiopian highlands.

The most significant feature of the landscape is the Great Rift Valley, which angles across the plateau. A string of lakes including Stefanie, Chamo and Zwai water the valley bottom. The plateau's largest body of water, Lake Tana, gives birth to the Blue Nile, which joins the White Nile at Khartoum.

For millions of years the valley has preserved the earliest traces of mankind, at Tanzania's Olduvai Gorge, at Kenya's Koobi Fara, and at Ethiopia's Denakil Depression, the lowest spot on the continent (512 feet below sea level on the shores of Lake Assal, just over the border in Djibouti). Here, in the basement of Africa, anthropologists discovered the oldest hominid species found up to that time, about three million years old. This adult female, about 3 feet 8 inches high, was dubbed Lucy, a name taken from a Beatles song popular at the camp.

About 1000 B.C., another woman loomed large in Ethiopian history, Makeda—the Queen of Sheba. The Bible states that when the Queen of Sheba

▲ *Ethiopian legend allows this young, fine-featured girl to claim the Queen of Sheba as an ancestor.*

▲ *Isolated pinnacles of rock called* ambas *are the characteristic landform of the jumbled Ethiopian highlands.*

33

heard of Solomon's wisdom, "she came to test him with hard questions." Satisfied that his knowledge and riches surpassed her expectations, she gave the king "a hundred and twenty talents of gold, and a very great quantity of spices, and precious stones." Solomon, too, seems to have been impressed, for he "gave to the Queen of Sheba all that she desired, whatever she asked." Then the queen and her retinue returned to Sheba, the present-day city of Askum according to Ethiopian lore.

Ethiopian legend fills in the gaps of the story. In particular, it embellishes ambiguous references to Solomon's gifts. The story tells that the day before Makeda returned to Sheba, Solomon threw a lavish banquet at which spicy dishes were served, then invited the beautiful monarch to his chambers. She accepted on the condition that he would not take her by force, and he agreed, provided that she take nothing without his permission. That night, thirsty from the spicy food, she took a drink of water. Solomon accused her of breaking her oath and seduced her.

Nine months later, Makeda gave birth to Menelik, the first Ethiopian emperor in a line that extended through 225 kings down to Haile Selassie. When he was grown, Menelik visited Solomon, studied

the Hebrew faith and the craft of statesmanship, and was anointed king of Ethiopia. Legend says that when Menelik returned home, he brought with him the true Ark of the Covenant containing the tablets of law God gave to Moses.

A Muslim variation of this legend refers to the queen as Bilqis, and locates Sheba (or Saba) in Yemen. Askum at the time of Solomon was not yet large enough to have produced a ruler of such wealth and influence as Makeda. But Yemen of the time was a powerful trading nation, and some specialists argue that the queen visited Jerusalem to secure markets for her kingdom's products.

Certainly a southern Arabian group called Sabeans did cross the "Arab Lake" (Red Sea) to settle in Ethiopia. Two groups emerged: the Tigres and the Amharas. The Tigrean language, Geez, derived from Sabean with its beautiful angular letters, ceased to be spoken about the tenth century. It survived as the language of literature until the 18th century, and still exists as the language of the church, even though most of the faithful cannot understand it.

The Tigreans and Amharas founded the Kingdom of Askum deep in the Ethiopian highlands. Until the last century, most of the emperors of the realm were crowned at Askum, in front of the St. Mary of Zion Cathedral. A princess named Judith destroyed the original building, and the Muslim conqueror Ahmed Gran, "the left-handed," leveled its successor in the 16th century. The present structure, probably built in the 17th century by Emperor Fasil, contains a magnificent collection of emperor's crowns. In the cathedral's holy of holies reputedly stands the Ark of the Covenant. No one is permitted to see it.

Opposite the cathedral, in a humble setting under the eucalyptus trees, stands a stone throne used down through the centuries for the coronation ceremony. From this simple relic it is difficult to imagine the mighty Kingdom of Askum, renowned as one of the "four greatest existing kingdoms of the world" according to ancient chronicles.

The imagination is aided somewhat by the most astonishing legacy of the Kingdom, the granite obelisks at Askum, each carved to simulate a multi-story building complete with false windows, arches and doorways. No civilization has ever carved such huge monuments out of a single block of stone. How the Askumites quarried, moved and raised such tremendous slabs of rock remains a mystery. The

tallest, now fallen and broken into pieces, was more than 100 feet tall—the largest monolith in the ancient world.

Only one stele remains standing, a shaft about 65 feet tall, representing a ten-story skyscraper. On the first level is a carved false door. Above, deep carvings suggest rows of grilled windows and stepped and recessed walls. It is likely that these strange monuments were erected by early Askumite kings in remembrance of the earthen skyscrapers of their original homeland along the Sabean coast in Yemen. The discovery in 1954 of caves beneath one of the monuments suggests that the shafts may mark royal tombs.

There are also several dozen stone thrones at Askum, scattered about in a state of utter confusion and abandonment. Apparently commemorative monuments, these thrones consist of huge granite foundations, surmounted by a seat, the only remnants of which are grooves where the back and sides were inserted. More than 2,000 years old, they probably belong to a "memorial throne" tradition that has its roots in the East.

These monuments, along with Askumite remains at Matara (undisturbed walls and staircases and an obelisk bearing one of the earliest examples of Geez writing) and at Yeba (a fifth-century B.C. temple with a majestic staircase) reveal the sophistication of Askumite civilization. The kingdom's Red Sea cities were key ports of entry for goods from the Orient. Egypt sent emissaries to the powerful emperors. King Zoscastes is said to have encouraged use of the Greek language (many coins from his reign bear Greek characters).

The Greeks wrote often of "Ethiopians" (the most wooly haired men in the world, according to Herodotus). The Romans drafted "Ethiopians" into the Imperial legions, and stationed them as far afield as England during the reign of Septimus Severus. St. Augustine called them "the blackest and furthest" of men and made them the symbol of his evangelizing.

The Greeks and the Romans, however, probably confused the Askumite Kingdom with the Land of Cush—the Nubian Kingdom of Meroe in what is now Sudan. It seems a strange mistake to make: the Ethiopian civilization was a power on a par with Rome, Persia and probably China during the fourth century A.D., when Europe gave the kingdom its most enduring and important legacy.

Around A.D. 330, Frumentius and Aedesius, two young Syrians from the city

▲ Matara: This bronze perfume pan, representing an ibex being attacked by a dog, dates from the fifth century, when the Kingdom of Askum was at its zenith.

► Askum: Monolithic burial monuments to royalty, these solid granite obelisks were carved to simulate the earthen skyscrapers of southern Arabia. No one knows how the shafts were quarried or raised.

of Tyre (now in present-day Lebanon) set forth on a journey to India. On their return trip, they were captured by pirates and taken as slaves to the king of Askum. History doesn't record the fate of Aedesius, but Frumentius converted King Ezana to a Christianity akin to the beliefs of the Coptic Church of Alexandria, Egypt. Ezana proclaimed the new faith the state religion, which it remained until 1974, when his descendant Haile Selassie was overthrown.

Following emperors embraced the gospel with fervor, possibly seeing it as a way to weld together the disparate and fiercely independent highland peoples into a single Ethiopian empire. The word was also spread by Byzantine merchants who did business in Askum. For a thousand years, Ethiopia developed in isolation, a Christian island in a hostile Muslim sea. Its Coptic brand of faith contributed to its split from mainstream Christianity. In A.D. 451, the Council of Chalcedon infringed the rights of Alexandria and Antioch as centers of Christianity, and the Patriarch of Alexandria withdrew to found a national church which professed the doctrine of monophysism— a "single nature" creed which denied the dual nature of Christ. Ethiopia became one of five churches of this type, the others being the Orthodox Coptic, Syrian and Armenian churches, and the Malankar Church of southern India.

Few monuments remain from the early Christian period. The most important is Debra Damo, a monastery overlooking the Tigrean plateau northeast of Askum. Za Mikhael, a sixth-century saint who nurtured monasticism in Ethiopia, discovered this site and decided to build a hermitage on it. The cliff was too steep to climb, so after three prayer-filled days and nights, St. Michael reputedly took pity on Za Mikhael, and ordered an enormous snake to carry him to the summit.

The snake lives on in the form of a stout leather cable that visitors (males only) must climb to reach the top of the *amba*. Here Ethiopian kings once exiled ambitious princes who might be tempted to topple the throne. Monks and priests also used the aeries to hide church treasures from 16th-century Muslim invaders.

On the spot where the snake deposited Za Mikhael stands Ethiopia's oldest church, which probably dates from the 10th or 11th century. Its importance stems from its construction, which represents a survival of the ancient style of wood-and-stone construction that Ethiopian architects used for a thousand years.

The walls are made of layers of dressed masonry and wooden beams with protruding round ends called "monkeyheads." Thirty-nine panels in the ceiling are decorated with animal and geometrical designs in the Coptic style. The monastery's 200 monks and postulants live in a village of flat-roofed huts, each containing a single monk. They catch rainwater in rock cisterns, and raise crops and oxen like any other villagers. Debra Damo's isolation has preserved a link between the architects and builders of pre-Christian Askum and medieval Lalibala.

▲ *Askum: These crowns worn by Ethiopia's emperor during the coronation ceremony come from a fabulous collection in St. Mary of Zion Cathedral. The crowns were fashioned from soft gold, perhaps from the storied mines of Ophir.*

◄ *All the statues of the Askumite period were seated on thrones. This stone figure from Haoulti, now in the Addis Ababa Museum, was once perhaps seated on a wooden throne and now must make do with this plaster replica.*

▲ *Askum: The sea-green reservoir poetically named "Queen Sheba's Bath" is not old enough to have been used by the beautiful tenth-century B.C. queen who charmed King Solomon.*

"I find it hard to write of such things, for I shall not be believed," recorded Father Alvarez, a Portuguese chaplain who was the first European to visit Lalibala, in the 1520s. No one did believe him, of course. It was only three centuries later, after other travelers had made the hazardous journey to Lalibala, halfway between Addis Ababa and Askum, that his reports about the village's astounding churches were vindicated.

This remote spot, situated at an altitude of 8,500 feet, owes its existence to the 12th-century King Lalibala, a Zagwe mountain warlord who seized power from Askum at a time of the old kingdom's weakness. He was eventually canonized by the Ethiopian church for his Christian zeal, a status that endured even after the Solomonic line retrieved the throne from the Zagwe tribe about 1270.

King Lalibala established his capital on both sides of a modest stream which he named Jordan, and proceeded to erect models of the monuments in Jerusalem, which was held by Muslims at the time and almost impossible to visit. The method of construction was remarkable: the complex of churches and chapels was carved out of the shoulder of a mountain.

The architects used two methods. For subterranean churches like Abba Libanos, they chiseled out a facade on a vertical cliff, then dug out a sanctuary behind it, as if it were a cave.

The second method treated four of the churches as monoliths. Artisans freed huge blocks of stone by trenching around them with primitive shovels, picks and adzes. The outside walls and roof were carved, then the freestanding, single blocks of stone were excavated to form

▲ *Lalibala: Only the roof of St. George's Church, decorated with three concentric crosses, can be seen here. The church, whose cruciform design is unique in Ethiopia, is actually 40 feet high.*

▶ *Lalibala: The 12th-century King Lalibala had a complex of churches and chapels carved out of solid rock. Only the facade of Abba Libanos Church is visible in this photograph.*

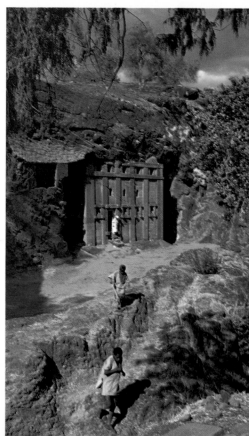

▲ Lalibala: Carved from a single block of stone, St. George's Church is reached via passageways excavated from the surrounding rock.

the church interiors, complete with columns, vaults, rooms and windows. Yet from base to roofline, each church is a single chunk of rock.

A network of subterranean passages tunneled through the surrounding rock led down to the church entrances. At Medhane Alem, for example, visitors emerge from a dark tunnel, far below ground level, into a small courtyard facing the reddish facade of a church 75 feet wide and 36 feet high. High above, the sky can be glimpsed.

Each church has its own character. The Church of the World's Redeemer, the largest, has five arched aisles and may have been copied from the ancient coronation church at Askum. Luxuriant paintings decorate the ceilings of the intimate Church of St. Mary, King Lalibala's favorite. The cruciform Church of St. George, just outside the village, is the most refined. There, sheltered in a clump of eucalyptus trees, is the roof, bearing three Greek-style crosses lying one within the other.

Ethiopia has some 14,000 churches, once served by more than 200,000 clergy. But at Lalibala, the Old Testament way of life of the Amharan people is more strik-

▲ *Lake Tana: Ethiopian emperors and priests preserved early relics of the church, like this processional cross and illuminated manuscript, by hiding them in isolated monasteries on islands in Lake Tana, northwest of Addis Ababa.*

▲ *Abba Yohanni: This cliffside cave church, one of hundreds in the province of Tigre, gleams with a fresh coat of whitewash. The church bears the name of its founder, believed to have been killed in a landslide.*

▼ *Guh: This fresco of Moses reveals an apparent Islamic influence on Ethiopia's Christian art. Some historians speculate that this figure originally wore a halo, later transformed into a turban.*

ing than anywhere else in the country. When it is time for evening prayer, the inhabitants of the village gather at the edge of the trenches surrounding the churches. The sounds of the *kabbara* (a liturgical drum) and the *sistra* (a rattle of Egyptian origin) rise from the sunken shrines until late into the night. Flocks of sheep graze beneath trees along the Jordan, where a cross commemorates Christ's baptism. Children drone prayers in Geez, a dead language incomprehensible to the faithful.

The rhythm of each day, like that of life itself, is controlled by the church. The complicated ceremony of baptism requires several priests. The child receives the name of the saint listed in the Synaxary (the book of saints' lives) for the day of the ceremony. A chain is placed around the child's neck, on which hangs a little silver cross which will be worn for the rest of his or her life. (There are 11 types of crosses with various shapes, including Latin, Greek and Star of David.) The male child is circumcised and is given a confessor. Finally, the child is led to church to take communion for the first, and perhaps

last, time. Only priests and other privileged persons regularly receive the holy eucharist.

Strict rules govern the lives of the clergy. Upon completion of his studies, the future priest is made a deacon and must contract a marriage. After 40 days, the union is declared indissoluble. After several years, the deacon is ordained a priest; he may then enter the holy of holies

and celebrate on the *tabots*, portable altars which represent the Ark of the Covenant.

Only monks take vows of chastity, thereby renouncing worldly aspirations and assuming legal nonexistence. It is said that some people become monks in order to evade creditors, who find it difficult to collect debts from monasteries deep in the jungle or perched on a sheer cliff. Unique to the Ethiopian church are the *debteras*,

◄ *Abba Yohanni: The interior of this cave church soars 30 feet high. The recent paintings on cloth that decorate the pillar on the left are in the style of early Ethiopian religious art.*

▲ *St. Gabriel's Church: Ethiopian artists have no compunction about painting over medieval frescoes. These brightly colored designs are of recent vintage, although the style is ancient.*

non-priests who are experts in reading liturgical song and are custodians of the church's traditional wisdom.

The Ethiopian year is punctuated by fervently celebrated feast days. *Maskal,* named for a yellow daisy that heralds the coming of spring after the heavy monsoon rains, commemorates the Invention of the True Cross.

Equal fervor is shown in other religious ceremonies: when priests are borne in procession, or when the faithful bathe in a ritual pool, set fire to a pile of eucalyptus wood, or mime Christ's entry into Jerusalem. On these special days, people wear pure-white *shammas,* a robe of white muslin bordered with colored embroidery and draped from the shoulder. Priests wear velvet coats embroidered with gold and silver and hold colorful parasols.

One of the most impressive ceremonies occurs on Good Friday. Priests spread rich ecclesiastical robes and rugs on the floors around the inner sanctuaries. In the sunken courtyard of the church, a covered log, representing Christ's body, is carried in procession around the walls. At one point, the priests fall upon a candelabrum, symbol of Judas the betrayer, and smash it with sticks and fists.

Exploring Ethiopia's remote churches requires a great deal of tenacity, for some of these shrines are almost impossible to

▲ *Christian holidays, such as this Palm Sunday celebration, are always accompanied by great ceremony. Clergy dressed in sumptuous vestments and protected against the sun by embroidered umbrellas lead the processions.*

▲ *Musicians and wandering storytellers, the* azmari *play* masiukos *(one-string fiddles) at all the festivites of Timkat (Epiphany).*

reach. The rockbound highlands are thought to shelter some 1,500 medieval churches; hundreds await discovery. It is interesting to discover that most of these churches are still in daily use.

The monastery of Abba Salama, for example, was located only in the 1960s. Its founder, Frumentius, who introduced Christianity to Ethiopia, became known in Ethiopia as Abba Salama ("Father of

Peace"). Seeking solitude in his old age, he retreated to a spot about 40 miles southeast of Askum and built a community just below the rim of a precipitous *amba*. Monastic tradition holds that the bones of the saint are on the premises. The roof of a cave carved in the cliff is supported by crude round columns, instead of the usual squared-off pillars, which divide the space into two aisles and

the nave of the classical basilica pattern. These suggest that the sanctuary was built in early medieval times.

The architects of these churches bequeathed to Ethiopia a rich legacy of ecclesiastical art and architecture. The church of Enda Abuna Yemata, carved into a majestic stone pinnacle in Tigre province, contains brilliantly colored frescoes, dating from the 16th century.

At the underground church of Dabra Abuna Aaron, sunlight illuminates the gloomy interior for only a few minutes each day through a hole in the rock roof. Priests use the brief light to read from the Scriptures. Monks claim that water never enters the hole during the rainy season. The church also contains a rare wooden crucifix; most processional crosses in Ethiopia are of metal.

▲ *Lalibala: On Christmas morning, priests and deacons cluster around one of the sunken churches here to proclaim the birth of Christ. Their chants are accompanied by the jingle of the* sistrum, *a rattle common in ancient Egypt.*

45

The most majestic monastery church in northern Ethiopia is Abba Yohanni in Tegre, which boasts an interior 30 feet high, crowned by ten preserved cupolas. In northeastern Tegre, a crude cliffside facade signals the location of Enda Mikael (St. Michael's). Behind the facade is a miniature basilica, 22 feet square, blending Askumite details with arches, vaults and dome from Byzantine Christianity. This strange hybrid, probably built in the late Middle Ages, was partly erected using traditional methods and partly carved from the side of the mountain.

Since the 1960s hundreds of churches have been discovered, or rather, rediscovered. The Jesuits knew of their existence in the 16th century, but that knowledge was lost for centuries. Each new discovery of a church is carefully recorded in Geneva by Roger Sauter, a Swiss teacher who once worked in Asmara. Experts claim there are hundreds more rock churches awaiting their first foreign visitors.

During the Crusades, tales of a Christian empire known as the "Kingdom of Prester John" tantalized Europeans fighting to free the Holy Land from Muslim rule. After the fall of Edessa (Mesopotamia) in 1144, a legend that originated near Cologne, Germany, began to spread throughout Europe. It told of a black African monarch named Prester John, heir to the Magi, who ruled a Christian state that would deliver Jerusalem from the followers of Allah.

Some explorers searched for the realm in the lands of the Moguls, but found only isolated Nestorians living on the Russian steppe. The kingdom was then rumored to be in Africa, beyond Nubia.

It was during the great age of European exploration that legend finally yielded to fact. The first accurate information about Ethiopia, which seemed to match the description of the Kingdom of Prester John, reached the West in the early 15th century. First, there were the accounts of Italian adventurer Pietro Ranzano; then, in 1441, two Ethiopian monks went to Italy to attend the Council of Florence; Finally, around 1478, Portuguese explorer

Piero da Covilham succeeded in reaching Ethiopia. The monarch of the time, Empress Helen, sent da Covilham back to Portugal with a request to King John II for an official embassy in Ethiopia.

In 1520, Ethiopia received its most avid chronicler, Francisco Alvares, chaplain to the Portuguese embassy. Passionately interested in antiquities, Alvares spent six years in the country, writing incredulous accounts of the strange world he encountered, including the fantastic rock churches of Lalibala.

He was aided in his explorations by da Covilham, whom the king had dispatched to divert the lucrative spice trade from Venice to Lisbon. Da Covilham had been "detained" by the Negus (King) Lebna Dengel, and had married an Ethiopian.

The negus might have also placed Alvares and his companions under house arrest, but the Muslim threat outside his borders called for diplomacy. In 1526 the monarch allowed the Portuguese mission to return home, but he refused to sign a mutual defense and trade treaty since the

▲ *At religious feasts, like this Epiphany celebration, the clergy do more than just sing hymns: They dance to the rhythm of* sistra *and drums.*

Portuguese had not delivered the guns he had requested.

The negus may have regretted his decision, for the following year, 1527, he found himself confronting Ahmed Gran, the "Left-handed," and his horde of Somali and Afar tribesmen and Turkish troops. For the next decade, the dreaded "scourge of Allah" ravaged the countryside, destroying churches and massacring the Christian population, while the negus and his court hid out in the remote monasteries of Tigre.

Realizing his error, the negus tried to renew contact with Europe, but he died before seeing the Portuguese land at the Red Sea port of Massawa in 1541. A contingent of 400 men battled alongside Christian troops from Ethiopia. The European force was reduced to 200 soldiers by the time the Battle of Waina-Dega was fought in 1543 near Lake Tana. Portuguese and Ethiopian forces routed the Muslims. Gran killed himself on the battlefield rather than accept defeat at the hands of the infidels.

Islam took its revenge in 1557, when Turkish troops occupied Massawa. Cut off from the Red Sea, Ethiopia again withdrew into the mountain fastness of its central plateau citadel while waves of Muslim invaders washed over the surrounding lowlands.

This isolation became total when the negus expelled the Jesuits from his realm

▲ *Fetching water in Ethiopia is a monotonous and never-ending task, usually performed by women.*

▲ *Blue Nile Canyon: Flowing out of Lake Tana, the river (here, a chocolate brown from suspended sediments) has carved a mile-wide gorge through the Ethiopian highlands.*

47

in 1633. The Society of Jesus had accompanied the earliest Portuguese missions, but they returned home from Massawa after buying their release from their Muslim captors.

The Jesuits received a mixed welcome. They landed in Ethiopia determined to re-ordain the clergy, re-baptize the faithful, and above all, suppress such ancient Coptic rites as circumcision and the use of Geez as the language of the church.

A Spanish Jesuit, Father Paez, succeeded in converting the Emperor Sousenios to Catholicism. But in 1626, Paez's successor, Father Mendez, went too far. He demanded that the faithful renounce the Monophysite doctrine. There was an immediate and massive protest by the clergy, the emperor's family and the population. In the face of this turmoil, Sousenios abdicated in favor of his son, Fasiladas, who broke off all relations with Rome. He restored the rites of the Coptic religion and expelled the missionaries.

In their own way, however, the Jesuits had helped to strengthen the Christian nation by enabling it to withstand Islam. The missionaries had encouraged education and scientific research, and had reformed a clergy that had become lax. Their fatal error was pushing too quickly for change in an unchanging land.

For centuries Ethiopia's emperors had moved their seats of government to keep regional dukes in line. "The capital is

▲ *Gondar: Black-eyed cherubim, upright and upside-down in alternating bands, decorate the ceiling of Debra Berham Selassie Church.*

▲ *Gondar: The imperial capital until the 19th century, this city has a complex of turreted castles with crenelated walls. Emperor Fasil, who built this structure in the 17th century, may have employed Portuguese artisans.*

wherever the negus pitches his tent," wrote one Portuguese traveler. Fasiladas and his successors established a more permanent capital at Gondar, and the city retained that role until 1855. There, in the rolling hills 30 miles north of Lake Tana, the emperors raised wondrous castles unique to Africa.

The earliest was built by Fasiladas soon after he expelled the Portuguese, although some scholars think the king used Portuguese artisans to complete the turreted structure. The castle seems to contain a mix of architectural traditions: ancient Askumite designs, Moorish and European influences, and similarities to the great castles of southern Arabia being constructed at that time. The Italians restored the stronghold during their invasion of Ethiopia, installing electricity and using the castle as their headquarters during their five-year occupation.

Also here is an 18th-century palace known as Ras-Beit, built for a Tigrean lord named Ras Mikael Sehul. It has been occupied by the lord's descendants continuously since its construction. Nearby is the Bath of Fasile, and outside of town stand the monastery and ruined palace at

Qusqwam and the 300-year-old church of Debre Berhan Selassie with its brightly painted roof and walls.

Gondar was long a forbidden city to Europeans. The emperors lived there in luxury, building baths for their princesses and concubines, decorating private quarters with mirrors and ivory furniture, and throwing up enormous crenelated walls pierced with gates.

Instead of moving the capital to quiet restive princes, the ambitious royal nephews themselves were moved—banished to an enormous *amba* called Wahni, which rose from the depths of a crater east of Lake Tana. The site was so forbidding and remote that 16th-century emperors hid the treasures of the kingdom there to save them from falling into the hands of invading armies.

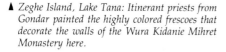
▲ *Zeghe Island, Lake Tana: Itinerant priests from Gondar painted the highly colored frescoes that decorate the walls of the Wura Kidanie Mihret Monastery here.*

Today libraries, barracks, audience halls and palaces in more or less dilapidated states can be seen peeking through the dense undergrowth on the outskirts of the modern town of Gondar, built by the Italians during their short-lived occupation.

The Wahni's fortified ramparts contrast with the idyllic setting of the 40-odd islands that dot Lake Tana. Thick with lush vegetation, these islands served as retreats for the royal retinue during times of crisis. Emperors would also visit the islands to implore for the intervention of

saints in times of famine, or to pray to a particularly valiant ancestor for victory in military campaigns.

About a dozen churches and monasteries are on the islands, some of them housing the tombs of kings and queens. Now that the decorations of the Gondar palaces have disappeared, the frescoes of Lake Tana churches are the only vestiges of this rich era of Ethiopian civilization.

The few existing manuscripts give only a vague idea of the great decorative cycles of Ethiopian art. (The finest, dating from the early 15th century, is preserved in the

monastery on the Island of Kebran.) The paintings of the so-called Gondar School show that, despite Ethiopia's isolation, sporadic contact with the outside world allowed new influences to be assimilated with earlier designs from 11th- and 12th-century Armenia and Syria. Elements of a late-Egyptian style can be seen in the bright red colors of St. Theodore's vestments and in the white charger of St. George.

The archaic works on these ancient pages are characterized by simplified figures, geometrical patterns, and a

◄ *Lake Tana: Many of the 40-odd islands that dot the milky waters of this immense lake, larger than Lake Geneva, support ancient monasteries and churches.*

▲ *Lake Tana: Many churches, such as this one at Nargha Selassie, are overgrown with the lush vegetation of the islands in this lake.*

51

distinctive way of interpreting religious themes. In a crucifixion scene, for example, a lamb replaces the figure of Christ—an image found nowhere else.

Influences from farther afield also made an impact on the church frescoes. Since Portuguese and Italian artists lived in Ethiopia during the 15th century, all the Madonnas painted after that date are flanked by the archangels Gabriel and Michael. In the 17th century, in response to a change in Italian artistic tradition, Ethiopian illustrations show the Madonna bearing the infant Jesus on her left arm, instead of on the customary right arm.

These frescoes are arranged in strict order, with the viewer starting the cycle from the east wall (Ethiopian churches were always aligned toward the east). The painting is inscribed with a long list of patriarchs and prophets, as well as representations of Old Testament events as related to the New Testament. Daniel in the lion's den and Jonah in the belly of the whale are shown as episodes foreshadowing the resurrection of Christ.

The south wall is decorated with portraits of the apostles and scenes from the life of Jesus, including the Visitation and the Last Judgment. The west wall bears the most important themes: the Coronation of the Virgin, the Virgin and child, the Crucifixion, and a procession of local saints accompanied by St. George.

Copies of these paintings, designed to teach the unlettered faithful, were widely disseminated by traveling artists. Unfortunately, many of these early replicas have been painted over, often systematically. Even today, it is not uncommon to see a painter clumsily covering a 16th- or 17th-century decoration whose beauty and charm could have been preserved by restoration. But Ethiopian monks attach little importance to the aesthetic value of the paintings. In their eyes, the image is solely of didactic value.

The golden age of Gondar obscures an important event in Ethiopia's history: the invasion of the Gallas (now referred to as the Oromos). For even as the dominant Amhara group raised their splendid monuments and castles, the Islamic Oromos people were invading the Ethiopian kingdom.

Opinions are divided on the origins of these invaders, who now represent 30 percent of Ethiopia's population. Some historians believe that they came from southern Arabia and settled near Lake Turkana. Others think that they were native to southern Ethiopia. What seems clear is that they first attacked the eastern plateau (occupied by Somalis), then the southern plateau near Harar, before turning northward to the highlands.

The Oromos advanced and settled, advanced and settled, penetrating further with each successive wave. The descendants of Solomon decided their best hope against these nomads was assimilation. The Oromos also considered this strategy to their advantage: One of their proverbs states, "Kiss the hand you cannot break." Iyasu II, who reigned from 1730 to 1755, set an example by taking an Oromos woman as his queen.

The mixture of the Cushitic Oromos and the Semitic Amharas was volatile. Finally, in 1855, an Amharan leader named Kassa defeated Oromos forces and had himself crowned Emperor Theodore II. Theodore unified Ethiopia for the first time in modern history with a reign of terror that saw thousands of his countrymen thrown over cliffs or burned alive.

Theodore, however, overstepped his bounds when he imprisoned a British consul in 1864. Queen Victoria sent Sir Robert Napier of the Bombay Army to the rescue. Napier led 30,000 men, with their artillery carried on elephants, more than 400 miles from the Red Sea to Theodore's fortified mountain capital of Magdala.

There, the British troops defeated Theodore's army, most of which had deserted long before Napier arrived. The negus himself committed suicide as gunners bombarded the last gate. Napier destroyed the citadel and marched away, leaving the empire in chaos.

▲ *For centuries the Arusi, members of the Oromos tribe of southern Ethiopia, have erected carved headstones over the graves of their chiefs. It is often difficult to distinguish ancient monoliths from more recent markers.*

The empire was restored by Menelik II, who used Oromos nobles as generals in his campaigns to add the Islamic lowlands of Ogaden and Eritrea to the Ethiopian realm. In 1887 Menelik also moved his capital south, to Addis Ababa, deep in Oromos-held territory.

The emperor imported thousands of eucalyptus trees from Australia to shade his capital, whose name means "new flower." Fine modern buildings grace this city of more than a million, including the Parliament House, the Commercial Bank and the Ministry of Foreign Affairs. An Italian architect designed the Africa Hall, where the charter for the Organization of African Unity was signed on May 25, 1963.

Addis has the biggest and most colorful market in Ethiopia. Here, in the Mercato, vendors sell frankincense and myrrh, herbs that flavor the local beer, Japanese radios, and native crafts.

Also worth visiting is the tree-encircled St. George Cathedral, built in 1896 and the site of Haile Selassie's coronation in 1930. The Italians tried unsuccessfully to raze the church in 1937. Today it houses works by Ethiopian artist Afework Tekle, who also contributed the stained-glass window in Africa Hall.

▲ *Standing tall and faceless in a forest of cactus, this Arusi grave monument marks the site of a tomb. Although their Islamic faith prohibits all human representations, the Arusi sometimes erect these statues if the deceased was valorous.*

53

The winds of change have not blown as strongly in the more remote regions of the country. In Simien Mountains National Park northeast of Lake Tana, flat-topped *ambas* and high ridges are separated by thousand-foot gorges. This rugged, 87-square-mile sanctuary shelters several rare species, including the nearly extinct walia ibex. The rare gelada baboon feeds in troops of as many as 300.

Abijatta-Shalla Lakes National Park, one of the most important bird sanctuaries in the world, occupies a sheltered spot in the Great Rift Valley about 175 miles south of Addis Ababa. The park is an important stop on the migration routes of many birds from the northern hemisphere wintering in Africa. During January and February thousands of geese, ducks and other waterfowl can be observed here.

The Beisa oryx is the most common animal in Yangudi Rassa National Park, northeast of the capital near the Djoubti border. Zebras, greater and lesser kudus, waterbucks, klipspringers and the elegant dikdik also appear in great numbers. The refuge is watered by the Awash River, home to hippos and crocodiles.

One of East Africa's richest and least-visited game sanctuaries is Omo National Park, tucked away in the southwest corner of the country near the border with Uganda. Here the Omo River flows through a hot and humid valley quite unlike the cool highlands of Addis Ababa.

▲ *Mekele: In this town in Tigre, women still spin cotton by hand. It will be made into a garment lovingly dyed, woven and embroidered.*

54

▲ The mile-high plateau of central Ethiopia is cultivated year-round. The typical Ethiopian hut seen in the foreground is called a tukul.

►Blue Nile Falls: A few miles after it exits Lake Tana, the river tumbles 140 feet over this cataract, the first on the waterway's 850-mile journey to Khartoum, where Blue joins White to form a single Nile.

55

Clumps of acacias dot grasslands stretching to the horizon. Herds of buffalos, zebras and antelope inhabit the dry plains. Eland can be seen in herds of several hundred, along with giraffes and elephants and common savanna predators like leopards, cheetahs and lions.

One of Ethiopia's great scenic splendors heralds the birth of a great river. A few miles southeast of its exit from the waters of Lake Tana, the Blue Nile rushes 140 feet over a cataract known prosaically in English as the Blue Nile Falls; the Ethiopians have a more poetic designation, Tis Abbai, or "great river smoke."

The Nile carves a spectacular mile-wide canyon on its looping route to Khartoum, where it joins with the White Nile to form a single stream down to the Mediterranean. The canyon is the haunt of colobus monkeys, hunted illegally for their long black-and-white fur, and baboons preyed upon by rock pythons and leopards. The Nile gorge was finally spanned by a bridge constructed in the late 1940s.

Other remote areas reveal the diversity of this vast empire. The tribes of western Ilubabor Province, which juts into Sudan, are of Nilotic stock, a minority in Ethiopia.

These unusually tall nomads migrate every year between the highland plateau and the valley of the Baro River to pasture their herds of cattle.

Their homeland is another undisturbed realm of African big game. Oryx wander over the Bilen Plain in Harar Province in mile-long strings. They share the savanna with giraffes and rhinos, dikdiks and gazelles. Through this grassland runs the Baro, en route to the White Nile, farther west in the Sudan.

The lifeblood of Kaffa Province is coffee; the fertile region may have even given its name to the stimulating brew. Huge fig trees entwined with liana vines shade the coffee shrubs on the steep hillsides, and double as home to colobus monkeys and hornbills. The provincial capital of Jimma has a sprawling business district built by the Italians.

Asmara, the second city of Ethiopia and capital of the Eritrea administrative region, also has an Italian look. The city's character was reshaped during the 1890s, when occupying forces laid out its streets and erected its main buildings. The original settlement, the "native quarter," is now the site of the market.

The city again finds itself in the center of conflict, this time between the new Marxist regime of Ethiopia and the Eritrean People's Liberation Front. The fighting has exacerbated the plight of the 1.5 million Eritreans threatened with famine from decade-long droughts.

The suffering of the hungry and war-weary population obscures the city's treasures. The Asmara Archeological

▲ *Wicker-workers rather than architects, the Gurages weave the roofs of their huts like huge baskets, then turn the structure over and add circular walls.*

Museum houses an excellent collection of historical objects from the Askumite period discovered at sites in Eritrea and neighboring Tigre Province. And the Italian restaurants—Esposito, San Giorgio, Rino's and others—await better days.

The walled city of Harar is the only easily accessible "window on Islam" in Ethiopia, a land where the Muslim population is roughly equal in number to the Christian inhabitants. Over the years, Harar has considered itself a Muslim bastion against fellow countrymen who follow the way of the cross.

The best view of town is from the top of a hillock crowned by the the mausoleum of Ras Makonnen, father of Haile Selassie. Depending on the season, the surrounding land is bare and ochre-colored, or covered in pale green grass.

The site also clearly shows the walls of the city, slender and unadorned ramparts designed to restrict entry rather than to defend against attack. And towering above all are the two simple minarets of the Mosque of Djouma.

For centuries entry to Harar was forbidden to infidels. Then, in 1855, Sir Richard Burton, near the end of his epic African journey, managed to slip into the town in

▲ *The timeless task of fetching water is especially difficult in Ethiopia: Villages are usually built on the hills far above water sources.*

▲ *Harar: Citadel of Islam in Christian Ethiopia,
this ancient city is dotted with mosques and
minarets from which the muezzin summon the
faithful to prayer five times a day.*

disguise. His journals of exploration
reminded the world of Harar's existence.

Burton would probably recognize Harar
today, although some of the gates have
been walled over. The town retains its
network of white houses built around
central courtyards (an oriental design
unique in Ethiopia), as well as its winding
streets, small squares and two large
markets—one Muslim, one Christian.

The women of Harar wear bejeweled
necklaces and bracelets on their arms, and
dress their hair in a double knot if they
are married. Their fingers are stained with
henna, their cheeks are rouged, and they
wear a flower over their foreheads or
behind their ears—a rare form of ostenta-
tion among Muslim women. In fact, a
form of matriarchy has survived here, also
quite exceptional in Islamic countries;
women can own their own goats and keep
the money they earn from the sale of khat.

The income derived from this plant
must be considerable, judging by the
number of men lolling about with glazed
eyes most afternoons. Legally grown and
usually sold fresh at the markets each
morning, leaves of khat plants are chewed
for their mildly stimulating effect, which

▲ *Harar: Muslim women here are thought to have
among the greatest freedom in the Islamic world.
Instead of veils, they wear makeup and flowers
in their hair, own their own livestock and keep
the money they earn from the sale of khat.*

boosts the productivity of field workers. Consumed in quantity, the habit-forming plant produces euphoria. More than 8,000 tons of this prolific plant are produced in the region.

Mohammed once described Ethiopia as a "land of justice," and even considered fleeing there to escape his persecutors. His followers, however, were considered second-class citizens in the Christian kingdom for centuries. It was from Harar that Muslims set out in the 16th century to attack the Christians in the highlands. The spread of Islam in Ethiopia, though, owes more to Arab merchants who settled on the coast, rather than the Harari disciples, some of whom were converts from the Oromos people.

Over the centuries, local sultans took advantage of the weak Solomonic dynasty in distant Amhara and Tigre, and formed local kingdoms that stretched from the shores of the Red Sea to the eastern flanks of the Great Rift Valley. The strongest link in this chain was Harar, firmly planted on the slopes of the Amhar mountains, where the the highlands meet the desert. It was not until the late 19th century when Emperor Menelik II repelled a Mahdist

invasion from the Sudan and captured the province of Harar that Muslim power was finally neutralized.

Muslims nevertheless retained political influence, which the Italians and the British utilized during the Second World War to offset Amharan power. Unlike Christian communities, however, the Islamic constituencies never banded together into a cohesive power base.

Harar reflects this divergence. Hararis, Oromos, Somalis and Arabs form independent communities within the city walls, each with its own elite, schools, associations and rites. Furthermore, the Islam here embraces animist beliefs.

The independent Muslims of Harar show a distinct disinterest in making pilgrimages to Mecca, which lies only 250 miles away across the Red Sea. This attitude seems to apply to all the faithful, whether they follow the Shaf'ite rite (Oromos and Somalis), the Malekite rite (Eritreans), or the Hanifite rite of the coastal communities.

Ethiopia is filled with pockets of "forgotten" peoples and places. It was only in the early years of this century that ethnologists discovered the existence of

such Nilotic tribes as the Nyangatoms of the lower Omo Valley, whose society was described as "teetering on the threshold of the neolithic"; or the Falashas of the northern highlands—the black Jews of Ethiopia.

The legendary descendants of the biblical Ham, the fierce, proud Afars—also called Danakils—claim as their realm the Danakil Depression, lowest point on the continent. Here, almost 400 feet below sea level, temperatures can reach 120°F, and the sole source of water for the meager vegetation that supports the goats and camels of 200,000 Afars is the intermittent flow of the Awash.

For centuries the Afars have mined surface salt from this forbidding region. At times the precious commodity was worth more than its weight in gold. The salt is dug out, shaped into blocks with axes, then loaded on camel caravans, donkeys and mules for delivery to villages in Tigre. From there, trucks deliver the salt throughout East Africa. Meanwhile, brine bubbles into each fresh cut, and the sun quickly evaporates it to produce more salt, renewing Danakil's inexhaustible supply.

▲ *Harar: In the winding lanes of this medieval city, Muslim women in brightly colored shawls stop for a chat.*

SUDAN

Africa's largest country—a third the area of the contiguous United States or ten times the size of Britain—is a sprawling potpourri of peoples, cultures and climates. The country is usually divided into the Arab north and the African south, but there are other, subtler distinctions in a nation that includes more than 500 tribes speaking more than a hundred languages.

The desert region, a vast realm extending south from the Sudan-Egyptian border to the capital city of Khartoum, encompasses most of the country's Arab population, which represents about 70 percent of Sudan's total of 22 million. Smaller tribes include the nomadic Hadendowa, the Bani Amir and the Rashwaida of the Red Sea area.

The steppe region from Khartoum west to El Obeid in central Sudan is covered with short, coarse grasses and shrubs, and populated by the Kawahlas, one of several tribes of Arab camel breeders. South of the steppe, the Nubas and Nuers live in a savanna of yellow grasslands. The area extends south roughly to the Sudd, a gigantic swamp that periodically floods an area the size of Maine. This seemingly inhospitable region is home to the cattle-tending Dinkas.

The equatorial region extends across the southern third of the country, home to Nilotic peoples like the Zandes, once fierce warriors but now a sedentary people living in the foothills of the high, green mountains; and the Lotukos farmers of the Imatong Mountains near the border with Uganda. These groups, some Christian and some still clinging to animist beliefs, are rich in tribal culture and folklore. Here, Sudan assumes its African character.

The Nile is the thread that binds this disparate land together in nationhood. The White Nile enters Sudan from Uganda, picks up tributaries from the highlands of the Central African Republic, then bogs down in the Sudd, where it meanders in a flowery labyrinth of floating islands of hyacinth—and loses 40 percent of its water to evaporation.

The river emerges from the Sudd and flows smoothly across the grasslands to Khartoum, dropping only 250 feet in 1,100 miles—about a foot every five miles. At the capital, it joins the Blue Nile, which

◄ *A single thatched door, secured by a pivoting stick, gives entrance to this traditional Nuba dwelling.*

▲ *Thread of unity in an immense land, the Nile enters Sudan as two distinct waterways: the White and Blue. The two branches join at Khartoum in the heart of the country, then flow as one to the sea.*

63

rises 900 miles away in Ethiopia's Lake Tana. Although a thousand miles shorter than the White Nile, the Blue contributes 70 percent of the water to the single stream that continues north. (During the dry season, the reverse is true, with the White Nile contributing 80 percent of the flow.)

The Nile picks up more water during the wet season from the Atbara River, an 800-mile-long river that also rises in the mountains of Ethiopia. It is the Nile's only tributary between Khartoum and the Mediterranean, 1,700 miles away.

The unifying force of the Nile has not always been enough to keep this restless country together. Independent since 1956, Sudan was wracked for 17 years by a civil war that pitted the underdeveloped African south against the Arab north, which has always controlled the country and until the turn of the century viewed the south simply as a hunting ground for slaves and ivory. At least half a million

people died in the conflict until President Gaafar Muhammed Nemeiri ended the strife in 1972 by granting regional autonomy to the south.

In 1969, Major General Nemeiri came to power in a military coup with the aid of the Soviet Union. Two years later a leftist attempt on his regime failed, and Nemeiri broke off relations with the Soviets; that same year he became president. Another coup, in 1976, which the Sudanese claim was engineered by the neighboring Libyans, drove the country into the Western camp. Today, Nemeiri keeps Sudan together by the force of his personality as he strives to create a nation that is "democratic, socialist and non-aligned."

The first references to the Sudan are all Egyptian: a bas-relief at Wadi Halfa, for example, celebrating the victory of a First Dynasty pharaoh over the Nubians, and the Palermo Stone, relating a Fourth Dynasty campaign against the Sudanese.

At the end of the Old Kingdom of Egypt, around 2200 B.C., a new people arose in what is now northern Sudan. They made black clay pottery decorated with geometrical patterns and at Kerma, just south of the Third Cataract, built a fortress, a palace, a funerary chapel and a necropolis, where archeologists discovered the tombs of princes buried with as many as 300 wives and servants.

Some archeologists believe that Kerma flourished as an independent realm, trading with Egypt until the Hyksos toppled the Middle Kingdom about 1800 B.C. The people of Kerma allied themselves with the Hyksos, but once Egypt ousted its invaders, the pharaohs turned on Kerma, razing its temples and pushing south to the Fourth Cataract, where Tuthmosis founded Napata around 1400

B.C. This was the farthest upstream that the ancient Egyptians ever reached.

Nubia, or the Land of Kush, became an Egyptian province and the source of the pharaohs' gold. The Egyptians erected small fortresses to protect the mines, and monarchs of the early Eighteenth and Nineteenth dynasties (about 1600-1300 B.C.) erected monuments to their glory. Queen Hatshepsut built at Buhen and Faras, Ramses II at Nepata, and Tutankhamun at Kawa. The monotheistic Akhenaten erected two temples at Sesebi.

An independent Kingdom of Kush arose about 800 B.C. Superb horsemen, Kushite warriors conquered the army of occupation, and subdued Egypt itself, then in a state of anarchy. The Nubians founded the Twenty-fifth Dynasty, often called the Ethiopian Dynasty.

The Nubians ruled from Thebes, adopting the pharaohs' ponderous style of architecture but spurning their ostentatious burial customs in favor of relatively simple interment back in Sudan. Nubian monarchs who chose to mark their graves (which often attracted robbers) usually settled for a modest brick pyramid, no more than 40 feet tall, with steeply sloped sides edged in stone.

▲ *The crude images on this whitewashed wall fronting a Nubian home include daggers and buses, as well as the scorpion, whose role is to protect the inhabitants.*

Nine important archeological sites from the kingdom have been discovered along the Nile between the Egyptian border and Khartoum. The most impressive is at Meroe, once the Kushite capital. Three burial grounds dotted with small pyramids mark the resting place of 34 kings, five queens and two princesses. The ruins of the royal palace and the great temple of Amun have also been discovered nearby.

Excavations began in 1909 and continue to shed light on this little-known era. (The Meroitic language has still not been deciphered.) One unusual find: the colossal bronze head of the Roman emperor Augustus, found on the threshold of a chapel in the palace. It must have been brought back from a raid around A.D. 24 against the Roman garrison stationed at Elephantine Island near the First Cataract.

The Kingdom of Kush flourished until about A.D. 350, when it may have been toppled by the Kingdom of Askum, based in present-day Ethiopia. The medieval kingdoms of Nubia, Maquarra and Abodia, which flourished in northern Sudan, were converted to Christianity in the sixth century.

The city of Faras, about four miles south of the Egyptian border, had long been an important center of early Christianity in the Sudan. But it wasn't until the 1960s, when a team of Polish archeologists worked feverishly to complete excava-

tions before the site disappeared forever under water backed up by the Aswan Dam, that the most sensational collection of early Christian paintings in the Nile valley came to light.

In Egypt, Coptic artists worked on dry plaster rather than using the fresco technique, hence the lamentable condition of many of the paintings. At Faras, however, the paintings were in a remarkable state of preservation. Inside a triple-naved basilica on the west bank of the Nile, artists worked between the eighth and the 11th centuries, decorating the capitals of the church's many pillars with Egyptian palm leaves and acanthus leaves of Greek design. More than 100 paintings in the cathedral included wide-eyed apostles, St. Anne, the Archbishop Ignatius, the Madonna with Bishop Marianos, a tondo (circular painting) of the Madonna, and a remarkable Nativity scene with the Magi on horseback. The treasures of Faras were divided equally between the Khartoum National Museum and the National Museum in Warsaw.

The Christian kingdom lasted until 1372, when Islam triumphed. (Another Christian bastion farther south held out until 1504.) The infiltration of Arabs from southern Arabia, which began in the eighth century, was peaceful. The newcomers intermarried with Nilotic tribes, who were then converted to Islam. Farther south, other Nilotic peoples

remained Christian and animist, creating the division that would embroil the Sudan in civil war some 12 centuries later.

In 1820, the Sudan was conquered again by Egypt, by a ruthless general named Mohammed Ali. He founded the capital at Khartoum in 1823, and established a Turkish-Egyptian regime that brought the country into the modern era.

▲ *Naqa: Ornate gateway to nowhere, this temple facade from the Kingdom of Kush combines Egyptian, Greek and Roman designs.*

▲ *Meroe: Crumbled by the winds of time, ancient pyramids cover the burial sites of kings at this ancient capital.*

Sixty years later, Sudan revolted against foreign domination. In 1881 a religious leader called the Mahdi, Mohammed Ahmed, began to preach in favor of a holy war against "the Turks," as all foreigners were called. The Mahdi and his motley followers captured the town of El-Obeid and wiped out the Egyptian expeditionary force of Hicks Pasha.

► *Mouawarat: The Meroitic god Sebiomekar is depicted, Egyptian-style, with a goatee.*

67

Major General Charles George "Chinese" Gordon was dispatched in 1885 to Khartoum to suppress the revolt. He was beseiged by the Mahdi's followers, and before a relief force arrived, Khartoum fell. Gordon died on the steps of his residence, a spear through his heart.

The Mahdi established the first Sudanese government in Omdurman, across the river from Khartoum, and preached the coming of the Kingdom of God on earth. His program was revolutionary: abolish all tribal loyalties, the Order of Dervishes, witchcraft and drugs; pay taxes voluntarily; give the state treasury all war booty; and follow a strict Islamic moral code.

The oppressive Islamic state lasted 13 years, but its philosophy has influenced all subsequent nationalist and reformist movements in Sudan. It was the first government to bring together the diverse peoples of the region, a step on the long road to nationhood.

Lord Kitchener, sent by the British in part to avenge Gordon's death, defeated the Sudanese at the Battle of Omdurman in 1898, and inaugurated the era of the Anglo-Egyptian Condominium, an uneasy alliance that governed Sudan until its independence in 1956.

Today the grand Union Jack design Kitchener laid out for Khartoum is lost amid urban sprawl. The Khedive's palace, across the river in Omdurman, now houses mementos of Gordon and the Mahdist forces, including battle drums, pistols and uniforms. The Mahdi's tomb, surmounted by his emblem of a spear-

pierced crescent, is the scene of colorful ceremonies on Islamic feast days, when torchlight processions wind through the narrow streets of the city.

Khartoum's sites include the well-organized National Museum, with its archeological treasures dating back to 4000 B.C., and the Natural History Museum, renowned for its collection of Sudanese bird species. But the most impressive site here is the confluence of the Blue and White Niles at Mogren's Point, below the terraces of the Hilton Hotel. From the Sunset Bar, the end of day is a spectacle not to be missed as the waning light suffuses the sky with delicate shades of pink, red and lavender.

El Gezira, the region that lies between the Blue and White Niles, is said to be the world's largest irrigated farmland — more than two million acres — growing most of Sudan's major export crop, cotton. Although its potential is far from fully exploited, El Gezira is the country's richest agricultural area, yielding crops of sorghum, wheat and millet. Sugarcane is grown at the Kenenan sugar estate, one of the world's largest. A sugar refinery built by Arab petrodollars has an annual capacity of 363,000 tons.

The Sudan also has 30,000 head of livestock, the largest herd in Africa. In addition, the country produces 90 percent of the world's gum arabic, a substance used in pharmaceuticals, cosmetics, textiles and adhesives. Still, only 15 million of the country's 200 million arable acres are under cultivation.

Just north of the regional boundary that separates north from south lie the grey

and reddish granite peaks of the Nuba Mountains, home to the Nuba people. The Nuba are remnants of several tribes that once inhabited central and western Sudan, but retreated to these mountains about five centuries ago to escape the Arab invasion in general, and slave traders in particular. About a hundred tribes live here, keeping cattle and growing *dura* (sorghum) on terraces in the foothills and on the plains below.

Isolated by ridges and valleys, the tribes speak a bewildering variety of dialects and follow vigorous tribal customs. One pastime shared by all is wrestling, part of a harvest celebration called *sanda,* which also includes dancing, singing and copious consumption of *marissa,* a low-alcohol beer made from sorghum.

Wrestlers carry the honor of their hamlets into each competition. The village champion does no work all year. He spends his time training in the *seribe,* an enclosure made of thorns on the outskirts of the settlement, and building up his strength with a special diet of sorghum, sesame, sour milk and honey.

Between mid-December and the end of January, a series of *sandas* staged in various villages attracts people from all over the surrounding countryside, eager to celebrate the year's good fortune with a wild jamboree. Before leaving home, the wrestlers whiten themselves with ashes and shave their heads. (The powdering and clean skulls make it difficult for opponents to get a good grip.) Some combatants hang calabashes from the small of their backs; these prove the wrestler has not been thrown.

▲ *Wide like the Nile and packed to the scuppers, this ancient steamer paddles downstream on the great river through the heart of the Sudan.*

▲ *Napata: The Egyptian deity Amun appears here at the first capital of the Kingdom of Kush in the form of a ram protecting Taharqa, pharaoh of the Twenty-fifth Dynasty.*

The matches occur spontaneously all over the festival site, with a crowd forming around the combatants. The rules of the game are simple: the first to touch the ground with any part of the body except the feet loses. The winner gets a ride around the grounds, courtesy of his fan club, and a wildcat tail to wear around his neck. The champion's role is to assume an air of utter boredom with all the fanfare and adulation

When daylight fades, a blast on a kudu horn signals the end of competition. The festivities continue, with music, drinking and dancing in long, snaking lines. With the rising moon, the celebrants return home to their villages.

The Nubas live in dwellings as distinctive as their pastimes. Five conical huts capped with thatched roofs enclose a central courtyard that also does duty as a kitchen. Each of the mud cylinders has a function: granary, barn, storage room, bedroom and a grain-grinding room.

In one corner of the courtyard, a clay pot suspended by two antelope horns serves as a shower. To work the device, the bather tilts the pot and water pours out of a hole near the lip.

Described as a "horrible region of everlasting swamp" by British explorer

Samuel Baker, the Sudd was long an obstacle to exploration of the Nile's sources. Not that finding the "font of the Nile" ever aroused much interest on the part of the ancient Egyptians. They believed that the river's annual floods occurred when the god Khnum lifted his leg, releasing life-giving water stored beneath his sandalled feet.

The Romans were more curious. Nero sent two centurions to find the source of

the Nile, but they soon became bogged down in the Sudd, that vast maze of reed-choked waters buzzing with tsetse flies and 63 known species of mosquitoes.

Surprisingly, the Nuer and Dinka peoples have adapted remarkably well to the area. These Nilotic cattle-raising tribes move between the plains and the swamps with the seasons. The Nuers, noted for their tribal scars, live in thatched dwellings on humps of high ground in the

▲ *A python curls around the neck of this colorfully dressed young girl from the southern Sudan.*

▲ *Omdurman: The mausoleum of the Mahdi, a fundamentalist 19th-century Islamic prophet, makes this city across the Nile from Khartoum the historical and religious center of the country.*

► *Naqa (overleaf): Massive sculptures of rams border the processional avenue leading to the Temple of Amun.*

swamp during the wet season, and congregate in cattle camps along the edge of the Sudd in dry season. The Nuers double as fishermen during the dry season, catching tilapia, Nile perch and catfish, which they dry and market in the Sudd's few scattered towns.

The Nuer compounds consist of a large circular hut for the cattle and a smaller dwelling for the people. The women plant sorghum in mounds of earth arranged in neat patterns behind the huts.

The lives of the Dinka also revolve around their cattle. When a male enters adulthood, he takes a new name from a bull calf in his father's herd. Cattle are used to buy a bride, pay taxes and purchase the necessities of life, including meat and milk. Dried cattle dung provides fuel, and has the added benefit of producing a thick smoke that fends off mosquitoes. (Dinkas also smear themselves with ash and fashion mud caps to ward off insects.) The Dinka are particularly famous for their songs—invariably about cattle—and their dancing, in which they leap as high as they can "pogo" style.

The Dinka habit of standing on one leg while tending cattle gave rise to medieval legends about a one-legged race which early European chroniclers dubbed

◀ *This Nubian balances a basket of sorghum that weighs about 75 pounds. A "doughnut" of grass cushions the load, but the cargo presses so heavily on the skull that eventually a bump is left under the hole of the doughnut.*

▲ *Dwellings found in the Nuba Mountains of southern Sudan conform to a centuries-old design. The five conical huts surround a courtyard, with each room reserved for a separate activity.*

73

"Monopodes." The Dinkas were depicted in carvings over the doors of cathedrals, in the same way that pygmies were a favorite theme of Egyptian sculptors.

The Sudd also shelters a bounty of wildlife. Plovers, swifts, fish eagles, herons, egrets, and saddle-billed storks all find homes here amid the papyrus and elephant grass, feeding on abundant insects and fish. This is also the haunt of the strange-looking and rare shoebill, or whale-headed stork, unique to the swamps of Africa.

Other denizens of this dank realm include crocodiles, an unsettling number of snake species and the monitor lizard, which can grow to five feet in length. Buffalo and Nile lechwes feed on the abundant grasses during the dry season. The lechwe, or waterbuck, is an antelope with long lyrate horns that has made a special evolutionary adaptation. The inner surface of its elongated hoof is bare, giving it a good grip on slippery surfaces.

Today it is possible to sail by paddle steamer as far south as Juba, via a canal that was dug in 1899 and later widened. It must be constantly swept to keep it open, for in this sluggish stream vegetation like water lettuce, hyacinth and lily grow quickly.

Another attempt to subdue the Sudd resulted in the Jonglei Canal, designed to irrigate 400,000 acres and reduce water loss from evaporation by diverting 20

◄ Dressed in her finery, this young Nuba woman celebrates the harvest at the sanda festivities. A wooden plug inserted through a slit in the lower lip adds a special touch for the occasion.

▲ *The custom of the Nuba allows girls, after dancing to the rhythm of the drums, to select the boy of their choice.*

the vast Southern National Park, where amid gigantic trees and hip-high grasslands roam herds of up to 400 elephants, as well as numerous giraffes, rhinos, zebras, leopards and lions.

Dinder National Park, 300 miles southeast of Khartoum, is the African big-game reserve closest to Europe. A spectacular range of wildlife thrives in the rolling savanna grasslands and tropical forest. Various species of antelope are most abundant: the rare and magnificent roan antelope, the spiral-horned greater kudu, waterbuck, reedbuck, bushbuck, and many other varieties.

The marine gardens along Sudan's Red Sea shore near Port Sudan also attract a growing number of travelers. The fishing is outstanding, and glass-bottom boats take visitors out to view the watery wonderland of the coral reefs.

Thirty miles south is Suakin, a jewel of a ghost town well worth a side trip. The island's name derives from a romantic local legend. Seven beautiful virgins were sent by the King of Abyssinia as a gift to the King of Egypt. Along the way, the maidens spent the night on an island, where they became pregnant. To account for their misfortune, they claimed "Sawwa Jinn" — "a spirit did it!" Earlier in this century, one traveler described Suakin as "... a magic little town, a city of Arabian nights, fantastic, aloof... few can fail to be affected by the restful mystic charm."

For 500 years, this was Sudan's gateway to the Red Sea, until the modern Port Sudan opened in 1909. Turkish traders built its coral houses, now crumbling into ruin. Muslim pilgrims from Africa's hinterlands came to the port to book passage to Jiddah across the Red Sea.

percent of the Nile's flow around the swamp. Work on the 225-mile canal, which is two-thirds completed, was halted in 1983 after repeated attacks by Sudanese guerrillas, who saw the engineering project as another attempt by the north to dominate the south.

South of the Sudd is the homeland of the Zandes, subsistence farmers who live in scattered compounds along the southwestern border with Zaire. Before the turn of the century, this tribe developed a mighty military empire originating in the Congo basin. The British defeated King Gbudwe's warriors in 1905, ending the tropical dominion.

Two of Sudan's three national parks are located in the south: Nimule National Park along the border with Uganda; and

▲ Struggling mightily for the pride of their village, these Nuba wrestlers grapple under the watchful eye of the warden. Spectators cheer on their champion from the shade of a giant baobab tree.

▲ Bold designs enliven the exterior of this Nuba hut. Constant maintenance is essential to keep the mud-walled dwellings and thatched roofs in good repair.

► Nuba women dance in snaking lines at the tumultuous sanda celebration, which combines harvest feast, sports contest and dance party.

EGYPT

No other country's history has been so inextricably linked to the Nile as the land of the pharaohs. In fact, there would be no Egypt without the Nile. Ninety-six percent of the country's 48 million people live in the Nile's delta and valley, which represent only three percent of Egypt's land.

The river's waters nourish a thin green strip of land through the heart of sere deserts, and yield Nile perch weighing as much as 200 pounds. The river is also a highway for armadas of graceful feluccas; barges hauling clay pots, grain, cotton and other products from Upper Egypt; and scores of passenger boats stopping at the sites of ancient Egyptian temples.

The antiquities along the banks have been celebrated through the ages, but the river also passes through regions of surpassing scenic beauty, both natural and man-made. The Nile flows by small fields of vibrant green, rows of ramrod-straight date palms crowned with fronds, villages of mud-brick houses of deep taupe color, and massive cliffs at Abu

Simbel. And always, far in the distance or near at hand, stretches the empty desert that flanks both banks.

By 2300 B.C., Egyptian engineers had cleared channels through the previously impenetrable First Cataract near present-day Aswan, opening a gateway to the south and the treasures of Black Africa—slaves, ivory, ebony, incense, even pygmies for the amusement of the pharaohs and their courts.

The First Cataract also marks a change in language, culture and physical character of Egypt, for this is where Nubia begins. The resettlement of the Nubians dealt a terrible blow to villagers, who had been forced to move to higher ground in 1902, when the first Aswan dam was built, and again in 1912 and 1933 when the dam was heightened. The Aswan High Dam has completed the job, flooding all of Egyptian Nubia and part of Sudanese Nubia as well. The villagers have resettled in the Kom Ombo district, paying a heavy price for progress that mainly benefits other parts of their country.

◄ *Cairo: The El-Azhar Mosque, with its five minarets and 300 marble columns, is a seat of learning as well as a place of worship.*

▲ *Cairo: This sculpture in gilded cedar wood, part of the Egyptian Museum's golden horde of treasures from Tutankhamun's tomb, represents Hathor; the cow-headed goddess.*

▲ *'Saqqara: Egypt's oldest pyramid, just south of Cairo, was built for the pharaoh Zozer about 2600 B.C. Until that time, royal tombs were in mastabas—long, flat mausoleums.*

Ancient Egypt Begins at Memphis

Visitors to Egypt are often too awed by the grandeur of the Old and New kingdoms to discover the early manifestations of Egyptian civilization. Yet understanding ancient Egypt is indispensable in comprehending what came later.

Little is known about life along the Nile before the Old Kingdom. Cairo's museum of antiquities, the "memory of Egypt," contains exquisite examples of blue enamelware, cylindrical vases of diorite, porphyry and serpentine, spoons for cosmetics and animal-shaped spatulas of green schist—all dating from around 4,000 B.C. and all made without metal tools.

These forms of expression, which emerged during the murky pre-dynastic period, endured until the Roman occupation, about 40 centuries later. One outstanding example from this period is the Narmer palette, a shield-shaped plaque showing King Narmer of Upper Egypt striking a Libyan prisoner.

Some historians think that Narmer was another name for King Menes, the founder of the first pharaonic dynasty. King Menes united the "Two Lands" of Upper Egypt (the Nile's upper reaches) and Lower Egypt (the Nile Delta) about 3,000 B.C. and founded the Thinite Dynasty. Menes' capital was at Memphis, on land reclaimed from the Nile.

The city remained an important provincial town even after the capital was moved to Thebes during the New Kingdom. The site was abandoned during the early Muslim era. Today, nothing remains of the First Dynasty's palaces, built of bricks, wood and reeds, but several statues still stand at a lovely site amid the palm trees: a colossal figure of Ramses II; his wife, Nefertari; and an alabaster sphinx, recovered in 1912 from the murky depths of a nearby swamp.

Due west of Memphis, on the edge of the Libyan Desert, is Saqqara, part of the necropolis of Memphis. The most impressive structure here is the step pyramid complex of Zozer, unique in Egyptian architecture and the first large stone

structure in history. It was the work of Imhotep, the chief of works of Zozer, second king of the Third Dynasty (c. 2667-2648 B.C.).

The buildings are of white limestone, the first time that material was employed in ancient Egypt. The complex is surrounded by a limestone wall decorated with recessed and paneled buttresses and 13 mock gates: only one functioning gate pierces the rampart.

The step pyramid began as a *mastaba*, the traditional rectangular funerary chapel of Egyptian kings up to that time. (More than a dozen dot the sands at Saqqara.) Later, Imhotep added four more mastabas, one on top of the other, to form the stepped pyramid. On top of this superstructure was a square shaft, sunk into the rock to a depth of 90 feet. At the base of this shaft was an oblong burial chamber built of granite blocks. An entrance hole was sealed with a granite plug weighing 3.5 tons. Four underground passages and galleries surrounding the burial chamber contained the burial equipment. Some of these galleries remained uncompleted; others were faced with blue tiles.

The royal family was buried near the tomb in a series of shafts, some of which plunged to depths of 100 feet. Grave robbers made off with the funeral loot

long ago, but the mummy of a child in an alabaster coffin was found in one shaft. The foot of another mummy, found in the main burial chamber, is thought to be the sole remains of King Zozer.

One of the enduring fascinations about the complex is that it is a city of simulation, with stone art and architecture used to approximate earlier materials. When archeologists removed the outer facing on the walls of the complex in 1926, they were surprised to find ribbed Doric columns similar to those found in Greece 2,000 years later. These columns, in turn, are limestone counterparts of trees used as supports in primitive buildings. The small limestone facing blocks recall the ancient method of buildling with mud bricks.

Stone panels within the burial pyramid were painted red to imitate the color of wood. Ceilings are supported by stone beams dressed like wooden beams, walls are decorated with bas-reliefs approximating plaited reeds, and the corners are rounded to enable spirits to move about more easily.

There are also fake storehouses, but the provisions within were quite real. These pantries of the afterlife contained wheat, barley and figs, as well as more than 40,000 different vessels fashioned from alabaster, blue mica and red marble.

▲ *Abydos: This wall decoration from the tomb of Ramses II shows prisoners symbolizing vanquished tribes being paraded before the sanctuary.*

▲ *Saqqara: This was the necropolis for Memphis, the capital of Egypt's Old and Middle kingdoms. A statue of the departed king stands on the threshold of a false door, above an altar intended for offerings.*

Also on the site stands the Pyramid of Unas, the last pharaoh of the Fifth Dynasty. This was the first group of pharaohs to decorate the interiors of their tombs, and the pyramid here contain the oldest known hieroglyphic tomb texts. Inside the limestone structure are alabaster floors, limestone walls and granite columns in palm shapes.

To the northwest lies the Serapeum, the burial place of the Apis bulls. In 1850, Auguste Mariette was sent by the Louvre Museum to purchase Coptic manuscripts from the Egyptian Patriarch. When negotiations bogged down, Mariette amused himself by attempting to locate an avenue of sphinxes mentioned by the Greek geographer Strabo. Mariette bought a tent, a few mules and some equipment and started digging in the sands around Saqqara. After a year of arduous toil, he uncovered 134 sphinxes leading to the Serapeum, an underground necropolis where the bodies of sacred bulls were buried in sarcophagi of granite, limestone and basalt. This remarkable discovery was the beginning or modern archeology in Egypt.

The cult of Serapis was introduced to Egypt from Europe by Ptolemy, who was looking for a god that both the Greeks and Egyptians could worship. There was

▲ *Memphis: Its sightless eyes fixed on eternity, this alabaster sphinx is one of the few surviving antiquities from the capital of the Old Kingdom.*

► *Giza* (overleaf): *Rising 40 stories above the desert west of Cairo, the Great Pyramid of Cheops is actually taller than that of Chefron in the middle, which was built on a mound.*

a long tradition in the lands of the Nile of worshipping Apis bulls, who were considered representations of the god Ptah. Dead bulls underwent a 70-day embalming process, the same as pharaohs.

Mariette found 24 sarcophogi of Apis bulls at Serapeum, most of them looted and only a few containing so much as a handful of bones. One sarcophagus, though, was intact and its jewelry is now displayed in the Louvre.

Northwest of the Serapeum, Mariette excavated the mastaba tombs of Ti and Mereruka. Both men were ministers, Ti of the Fifth Dynasty, and Mereruka of the Sixth Dynasty. These large tombs are full of paintings of the ministers' lives as well as fine examples of Old Kingdom sculpture. Reliefs in the courtyard of the Ti tomb show scenes of pigeons, cranes and storks; the inner chamber is decorated with scenes of hunting and farming, and craftsmen at work.

King Snefru, the founder of the Fourth Dynasty (2613-2694 B.C.), built two pyramids at Dahshur: the regular-shaped "Red Pyramid," and the "Bent Pyramid,"

so called because the angle of its slope decreases halfway up from 50 to 43 degrees. The reasons for this strange design are so far unknown. Its obvious symbolism suggests the possibility that two monuments were merged into one. This theory is supported by the unusual presence of two entrances, 40 and 100 feet above ground, as well as two shafts and two funerary temples. Farther south, at Maidum, Snefru built a third pyramid which, having lost its facing and part of its base, now resembles the step pyramid at Saqqara.

Between Maidum and Giza, a distance of 50 miles, a veritable string of pyramids stretches across the desert horizon. In ancient times their polished surfaces reflected the rays of the sun, the celestial body to which the pharaoh's soul was drawn. The pharaoh's mortal remains, preserved for eternity by embalming, were protected by a granite sarcophogus deep within an immense mass of stone designed for conquering the heavens.

The largest is the Great Pyramid of Cheops, at Giza, which is oriented in such a way that indicates perfect geographical knowledge of true north. It covers an area of about 13 acres, measures 756 feet along all four sides, and stands 450 feet above the desert, although erosion makes exact measurements difficult. The rigorously exact dimensions of this monument, as well as those of Cheops' successors, Chefren and Mycerinus, are of real significance only to the mathematicians of fictional archeology, who claim to read the future of mankind in the stones.

Of greater interest is the age-old question of how these pyramids were built. Historians have had to resort to inspired guesses. The Greek scholar Herodotus estimated that to cut, handle and haul into place the 2.3 million blocks of limestone in Cheops' pyramid must have required 100,000 men working at least 30 years—including ten years just to build the ramp up which the stones were moved into position. The laborers probably only worked on the project three months of the year when the flooding Nile brought farming to a halt.

Archeologists agree on these basic facts, but the actual method of construction is still debated. It is known that the rough-hewn blocks were shipped down the Nile from quarries to the foot of the Giza plateau, then hoisted onto rollers and hauled up mud-brick ramps.

The pyramids of Giza must be studied from many angles at different times of the

day to appreciate their full effect: at sunrise and at dusk; under the dramatic illumination of the *Son et Lumiere* show; from the edge of the nearby cliff; from the Moslem cemetery, where the three pyramids appear to be of equal height; and from the summit of Cheops, with its magnificent view of the city, the desert, the Nile and its narrow strip of green—the "gift of the river."

A visit to the Great Pyramid (all three are open, but most people just visit the pyramid of Cheops) is an awe-inspiring experience, but not one for those suffering from claustrophobia. The air is stale, and the dimly lit corridors slope so steeply that visitors must walk nearly double. Then, if the thought happens to cross one's mind that untold tons of rock weigh down from above, it's not difficult to feel the cold breath of eternity brush one's cheek.

The present entrance to the pyramid of Cheops was hacked out of the north face. At the end of the narrow corridor is the Grand Gallery, 28 feet high and 153 feet long but only a few feet wide. This leads to the burial chamber, which houses the remains of Cheops' granite sarcophagus. Two air holes which extend to the top of the pyramid were designed to allow the king's *ka* (soul) access to his body.

Six additional pyramids were built alongside the Great Pyramid and the Pyramid of Mykerinus to house the remains of the families of the pharaoh's wives. In addition, many tombs of nobles are found in the Giza complex. A diorite statue of a pharaoh found in the lower temple of Cephron, known as the Valley Building, is now one of the treasures of Cairo's Egyptian Museum. This massive square temple has sides 150 feet long and granite walls 40 feet thick. Two entrances lead to the *naos,* where 23 statues of kings were discovered. The colossal square pillars and stone blocks that form the walls convey strength and austerity, somewhat softened by the shafts of light falling from openings in the ceiling which play, like spotlights, on the polished surface of the statues and on the alabaster paving stones.

Beside the temple five boat pits were discovered by archeologists over the years. These barges ferried the remains of the pharaoh from his capital at Memphis to the necropolis at Giza, and then were buried here on the site, ready for the voyage into eternity. Unfortunately, the pits were empty.

Archeologists have excavated the Giza plateau for so long that it seemed unlikely

▲ *Giza: Bathed in a ghostly glow, the Sphinx stands guard above the royal necropolis. Carved from solid rock, this 66-foot-high figure has been battered by time, neglect and foreign troops, who used it for target practice.*

► *Giza: More than 2.3 million blocks, some weighing as much as two tons, went into the construction of the pyramid of Cheops. The base of the 4,500-year-old tomb covers 13 acres.*

that one of these royal barges would ever be found. Then, in 1954, three pits were discovered south of the Great Pyramid. Two pits were empty, but the third contained a fully rigged cedar boat—the world's oldest. This discovery is now housed in a concrete and glass museum on the south side of the Great Pyramid.

Propelled by 26-foot oars, the 140-foot boat is made of cedar from Lebanon. It was found disassembled and many of its 1,200 pieces were marked with ship-wrights' instructions to permit reassembly in the afterlife. Buried in an airtight pit along with thousands of feet of rope, it survived 4,500 years until reassembled, not in another life, but in this one.

The road down the hill southeast of the Great Pyramid leads to the valley that contains that most Egyptian of symbols, the Sphinx, which has stared enigmatically in the opposite direction from the pyramids for the past 45 centuries.

After the overwhelming size of the pyramids, the Sphinx looks almost disappointingly small, a miniature. It was probably carved from a knoll left by the quarrying of stone for Chefren's pyramid. In fact, the sphinx probably bears that king's features, and was part of his valley temple complex. The Sphinx's nose was bobbed a number of times. Soldiers in the Mamlouk era (13th to 16th centuries) took potshots at it, and Napoleon's soldiers used it for target practice.

▲ *Cairo: The tombs of ancient Egypt have yielded many models of river craft which sailed the Nile in pharaonic times. This vessel, hung with a tattered sail, is in the Egyptian Museum.*

▲ *Luxor: Hidden behind these craggy sandstone bluffs is the Valley of the Kings, where the pharaohs and nobles of the New Kingdom were buried, including the boy-king Tutankhamun.*

► *Luxor: These monumental pylons, gateway to the Temple of Thebes, were decorated with six statues of Ramses II, though only these three mutilated figures remain. The mate to the obelisk on the left now stands in Paris.*

Thebes, the New Capital

At the beginning of the New Kingdom (1570 B.C.), the Egyptians chose Thebes as the ideal site for their new capital. Known today as Luxor, the city 420 miles upstream from the Old Kingdom capital of Memphis eventually became the chief city of Egypt, one of the capitals of the ancient world and a testament to Egypt's golden age. The grandeur of its monuments inspired Homer to immortalize Thebes as "the city of the hundred gates."

After the barren plateau of Saqqara and Giza, no one can remain indifferent to the landscape of Upper Egypt, where the Nile flows more slowly between wider banks. Feluccas glide by as in a dream. On the right bank, the land slopes gently up from the river. To the Egyptians, the eastern bank of the Nile was considered the land of the living, the place where the sun rose. The west bank was the land of the dead, where the sun set over the western desert. Here, funerary temples and tombs of kings were hidden in desolate gorges.

In the center of the modern town is the Temple of Luxor, dedicated to the Theban god Amun-Re. Several pharaohs contributed to the temple's construction, starting with Amenophis III in the 14th century B.C. He died before completing the work, and his son Akhenaten ignored the structure in favor of his own building projects honoring the god Aten. After Akhenaten's death, the Tutankhamun undertook to complete his predecessors' work.

◄ *Near Luxor: The Colossi of Memnon once guarded the entrance to the long-vanished temple of Amenhotep III. Legend says that the broken statues wailed at every sunrise until Emperor Septimus Severus had them restored.*

▲ *Necropolis of Thebes, near Luxor: In the second courtyard of the Ramesseum, the enormous temple of Ramses II, pillars represent the dead pharaoh as the mummy of Osiris, one of the principal Egyptian gods.*

▲ *Necropolis of Thebes, near Luxor: Half-hewn out of the cliffs, the Temple of Hatshepsut venerates a powerful female pharaoh who claimed divine birth. She raised colonnades, terraces and promenades to ensure her glory.*

Ramses II made his own additions in the Nineteenth Dynasty (1320-1200 B.C.), including the front pylon (ornamental gate) and the Peristyle Court. Before the pylon once stood six huge statues of Ramses, two standing and four seated, and two obelisks. The two seated statues and one standing statue remain, as does one of the 75-foot-high obelisks; the other was given to the French by Mohammed Ali in the 19th century and now graces the Place de la Concorde in Paris.

The Peristyle Court is surrounded by a double colonnade of papyrus-bud columns, 74 in all. On the second-story level of the colonnade is the facade of the Mosque of Abdul Haggag, which was once the original front wall and entrance. When archeologists started excavating the temple, this was the level of Luxor village. The townspeople insisted that the mosque stay, so the excavations went on around it. The mud-brick minaret stands on the stone lintel of the ancient temple.

Near the far gateway of the courtyard are two statues of Ramses II seated, with his wife Nefertari (at a much smaller scale) standing by his side. Other statues of a standing pharaoh are identified as Ramses II, but the sculptures were erected by

Amenophis III, the original builder of the temple. The egotistical Ramses scratched out his predecessor's name and added his own in its place.

Two miles north of Luxor sprawls Ipetesut—"most esteemed of places"— known to our era as Karnak. This vast complex of temples covers an area of 60 acres and took almost 2,000 years to build as a succession of kings added monuments to their own glory.

This was the heart of the cult of Amun, a diety who held a minor place in the Old Kingdom pantheon of gods. When the capital was moved to Thebes, he acquired the rank of an imperial divinity by taking on the qualities of Re, the sun god, under the name of Amun-Re. He was the creator of all other gods and had no end and no beginning.

In the immense temple of Karnak, other gods were represented merely for the sake of appearances. But virtually everything in the temple was dedicated to Amun-Re: the monumental pylons, colonnades, obelisks and sacred lakes. Pharaohs had their military exploits inscribed on the walls, in order to bask in the reflected glory of the god, but even the king knelt before Amun-Re.

▲ *Necropolis of Thebes, near Luxor: The profuse decoration of the Temple of Ramses III at Medinet Habu celebrates the pharaoh's brilliant military campaigns and his close relationship to the gods.*

▲ *Luxor: Reflected in the murky waters of the Sacred Lake, the sprawling Temple of Amun at Karnak is a vast complex of pylons, columns and obelisks erected by a succession of pharaohs over a period of 2,000 years.*

▶ *Luxor: In a tradition dating back 1,300 years to the Old Kingdom, a tiny statue of Nefertari is placed beside the enormous foot of her powerful husband, Ramses II.*

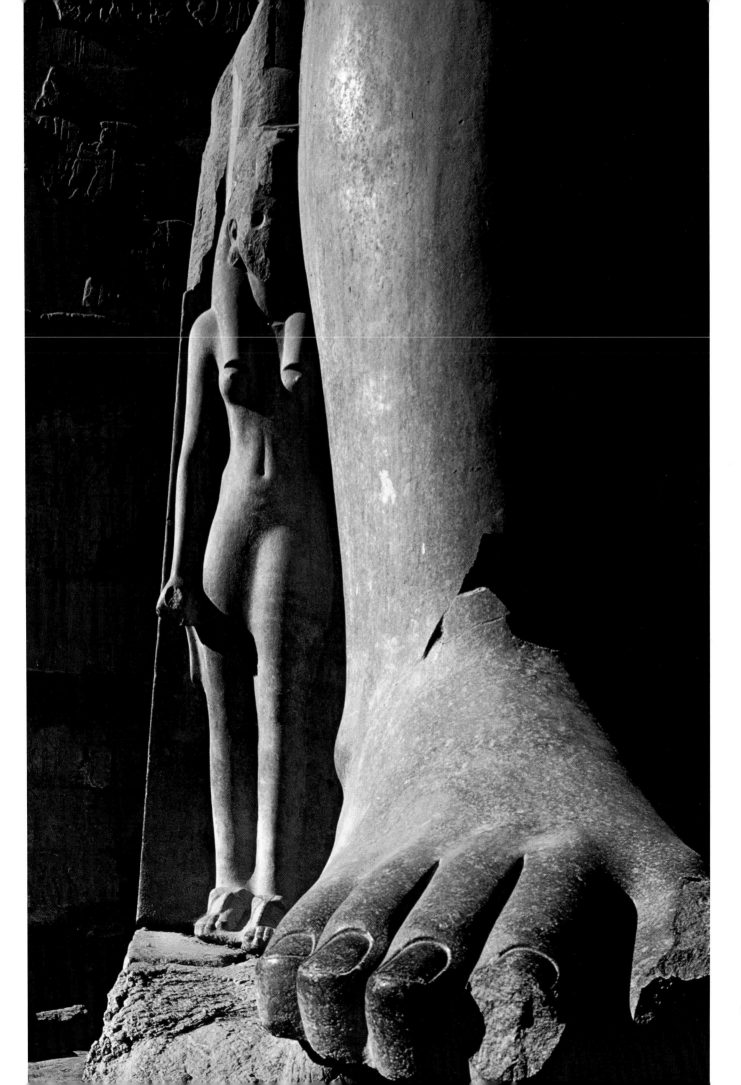

Each dynasty contributed to the Temple of Karnak, sometimes by destroying what predecessors had built. The overall plan is therefore not easy to grasp, especially since the center of the temple, built in limestone at the beginning of the Middle Kingdom (around 2050 B.C.), was razed to make quicklime from the stones.

This jumble of buildings is nonetheless extraordinarily beautiful and grand. A sense of one's insignificance and mortality is lent by the great Hypostyle Hall, where 134 columns, 70 feet tall, rise in tiers like a great stone forest. Columns upon columns upon columns—the sight dwarfs anything from ancient Greece or Rome. The conceptions of Egyptian architects "are those of men a hundred feet high," wrote French Egyptologist Jean-Francois Champollion.

Everything in the complex is oversize: the 40-foot-high statue of Ramses II, with the diminutive statue of Nefertari between its legs; the avenue of sphinxes leading to the first great pylon; the carved pink granite pillars of the ceremonial hall built by Tuthmosis III; the courtyard of Amenophis III, where Hatshepsut erected two obelisks (one is still standing; its mate graces the Place de la Concorde in Paris).

The inner sanctuary, built mainly around 1400 B.C. during the reign of Amenophis III, is more in keeping with modern ideas of orderly design. However the section added by Ramses II—the inner courtyard and pylon—is not in line with the older structures. The graceful peristyle, with its columns shaped like stylized papyrus bundles or parasols, stands out from the walls, on which are narrated the

▲▲ *Luxor: In spite of a taste for the monumental, the New Kingdom produced restrained statuary, like this serene bust at the Temple of Amun.*

▲ *Luxor: The great temple of Karnak was adorned with rows of ram-headed sphinxes during the reign of Ramses II.*

ceremonies of the feast of Opet, the goddess of fertility.

This mid-July feast was celebrated to greet the annual Nile flood. The statue of Amun was taken from the Temple of Karnak and placed on a ceremonial barge followed by three other craft, including one transporting a statue of the pharaoh. The procession sailed upriver to the Temple of Luxor, where the boats were carried into the sanctuary and placed in chapels. Ten days later, the procession sailed back downstream to Karnak. This was considered sufficient time for Amun to impregnate his celestial wife, Mut, a symbolic representation of the Nile floods which gave new life to the parched land. A curious variation of this festival exists today: At Luxor a Muslim feast includes a parade of a boat through the streets.

In the 14th century B.C., a heretic king named Amenophis IV ended almost 20 centuries of Amun worship and installed the world's first monotheistic religion. The Egyptian empire was still in its golden age in the 14th century B.C., when Amenophis III turned over control of Egypt to his son. The realm embraced large areas of the Upper Nile, as well as the eastern shore of the Mediterranean.

▲ *Luxor: Faceless guardians of the entrance to the Temple of Luxor, these 45-foot-high statues representing Ramses II wear the double crown of Upper and Lower Egypt.*

theon. In Amun's place, he elevated the Aten, the sun's disk, to the position of primary diety.

By the sixth year of his rule, Amenophis IV changed his name to Akhenaten, probably meaning "He Who Serves the Aten," and proceeded to consolidate his new god's authority by obliterating the name Amun from Theban monuments.

Early in his reign the pharaoh added still more monuments to the great complex at Karnak. His great temple, which may have extended more than a mile into the desert, rose east of the Temple of Amun. The structure stood for little more than 20 years. Then it was razed by later monarchs who cannibalized it as a source of building materials, including fill for the core of the Ninth Pylon, one of Karnak's massive ceremonial gateways.

About the time Amenophis IV changed his name, he also moved his residence from ancient Thebes to a new site 240 miles downstream at Tell el Amarna, which he renamed Akhetaten, "The Horizon of the Aten." There, with astonishing speed, he erected a new city cradled within circling cliffs, complete with luxurious palaces, public buildings, and another massive temple. This structure had no roof, except in the hypostyle hall, to allow Aten's life-giving rays to enter his sanctuary. For the first time, a necropolis was laid out on the right bank of the Nile, its perimeter marked out by boundary stones.

Though Amenophis IV apparently possessed a brilliant mind, his body may have been grossly misshapen due to some glandular disorder. He commanded his artists and sculptors to portray him truthfully. Slight variations occur in the statues that survive, but all depict the Pharaoh with a hatchet chin, slender neck, bulbous belly and thighs, and spindly lower legs.

About the time of his succession, perhaps at age 16, the future pharaoh married Nefertiti, whose name means "The Beautiful One is Come." One of the six daughters of this union would wed the boy king, Tutankhamun.

Cautiously at first, then later with surprising swiftness, the new pharaoh wielded his power over Amun, symbolic god-ruler in Egypt's crowded pan-

▲ *Luxor: The great hypostyle hall of the Temple of Amun at Karnak, which covers an acre, comprises 134 giant columns crowned by papyrus-bud capitals. A staff of 2,623 slaves once served the temple.*

► *Luxor: From Tuthmosis I (1525 B.C.) on, all the New Kingdom pharaohs added adornments to the great Temple of Amun at Karnak, including their own portraits.*

Armana was the site of one of the most creative periods in Egypt's long history. "Great in loveliness, mistress of pleasant ceremonies, rich in possessions," was how the ancient texts described it. The city's wealth of tomb art and inscribed stelae have given its name to the distinctive style of exaggerated naturalism that is the hallmark of Akhenaten's era. The most breathtaking example is the bust of Nefertiti, discovered in the ruins of a sculptor's workshop.

Preoccupied with cultural and religious reforms, Akhenaten neglected the affairs of State. Within 15 years of his coronation, Akhenaten witnessed the virtual collapse of his empire. His death, probably in his early 30s, followed soon after. The Egyptian court reverted to its polytheism, and the seat of power returned to Thebes.

◀ *Luxor (preceeding page): Master of the Temple of Amun during the Twenty-fifth, or Nubian, Dynasty (747-656 B.C.), the High Priest Pinedjen had a 50-foot statue of himself erected in the first courtyard.*

▲ *Luxor: Mutilated statues mount their eternal guard between the carved pillars of the Temple of Luxor.*

▲ *"Praise from the chief wife of the king, his beloved Nefertiti, living, healthy, and youthful forever and ever." This hymn to the god Aten from the favorite consort of the renegade pharaoh Ahknaton was made 3,300 years ago.*

Valley of the Kings

The glittering treasures found in the tomb of Akhenaten's successor and younger brother, the famous boy-king Tutankhamun, demonstrate vividly that Akhenaten's religious beliefs did not live long after his death. The powerful clergy returned Amun to his rightful place in the pantheon as god of Thebes and protector of the dynasty. The ten-year-old Tut was powerless to stop them.

When Tutankhamun died at age 20, he received a traditional burial in a tomb sunk in the craggy bluffs of the Valley of the Kings, across the river from Thebes. From the Eighteenth Dynasty on, the god-kings of Egypt were interred here, surrounded by their worldly belongings for the long voyage through eternity.

Sixty-two royal tombs have been discovered, almost all plundered long ago. The incredible treasures they once contained can only be surmised. Among the more

lavish tombs are those of Seti I, which contains more than 300 feet of corridors decorated with sculptures and frescoes, and Amenophis II, where the yellow walls are illustrated with scenes from the Book of the Dead.

The fabulous horde from Tutankhamun's tomb—a modest burial by ancient Egyptian standards—was recovered by English archeologist Howard Carter, who had teamed up in the early 1900s with his patron, Lord Carnarvon, to find out if any of the royal crypts rimming the Nile Valley had kept their secrets. In November 1922, Carter stumbled on one of the most extraordinary treasures in history, the nearly intact tomb of Tut.

There were nearly 5,000 items in all. A gold statuette of Amenhotep III, Tut's father, crouches in the attitude of a child, as though to express oneness with a dead son who would be reborn. (A lock of hair

▲ *Sheikh Abd el-Qurna: This modern village in the Theban hills near Luxor sprawls amid the tombs of the New Kingdom pharaohs.*

▲ *Luxor: A blue-faced Osiris from the tomb of Seti I in the Valley of the Kings wears the long, curving false beard that Egyptian art reserved for gods. Pharaohs were depicted with short beards.*

99

from Tut's mother, Queen Tiye, was also found in the tomb.) Three gilt funerary beds with animal-like sides seemed to Carter "uncanny beasts . . . almost terrifying." A chest of linen clothes rested on one bedstead decorated with a figure that is half hippo and half lion, representing Thoueris, patron of birth. Such beds may have held Tut's body while it was being mummified.

A life-size statue of Tut carrying the mace of rule and rod of majesty stood at the door of the burial chamber. Thin gold leaf covered the headdress, collar, kilt, bracelets and sandals. A wooden throne covered with sheet gold, silver, gems and glass bore winged cobras and lions' heads. Other treasures from the tomb include a writing case containing ink and reeds; golden knives in golden sheaths; alabaster drinking cups designed as half-open lotuses; a mirror in the shape of an ankh

▲ *Valley of the Kings, near Luxor: This barren valley gives no hint of the treasures that were interred here in more than 60 tombs of nobles and pharaohs.*

▲ *Valley of the Kings, near Luxor: The sarcophagus containing the mummy of Tut remained undisturbed for 3,200 years until archeologist Howard Carter discovered the chamber in 1922. The other tombs in the Valley of Kings had been pillaged.*

100

▲ *Necropolis of Thebes, near Luxor: Sennefer,*
mayor of Thebes in the 15th century B.C., spent
a fortune embellishing his cheerfully decorated
"house of eternity."

(the Egyptian symbol of life); tasseled earrings of gold, semiprecious stones and colored glass; and most exquisite of all, a translucent quartz scarab set in gold beneath the all-seeing onyx eye of Horus.

In all antiquity no one built more temples to his own glory than Ramses II (1304-1237 B.C.). A forest of obelisks and colossi from the Delta to Nubia celebrated his renown.

In 1271 B.C., according to legend, Ramses and his troops held a large army of Hittites at bay in the Battle of Kadesh (in present-day southern Syria) until the arrival of the main Egyptian army. "I have whitened the plain of Kadesh with their bones and, before their number, none knows where to tread," records the pharaoh's official account.

A heroic representation of what was more a successful retreat than an overwhelming victory decorates the walls of Ramses' astounding temple to himself, hewn out of the imposing cliffs at Abu Simbel, 180 miles upstream from Aswan.

The chief palace architect directed

construction. Surveyors laid out the axis of the Great Temple so that the rising sun's rays would strike 180 feet back into the inner sanctuary, illuminating figures of the god Amun and the god-king Ramses each mid-February and mid-October. Just to the north, surveyors planned the Small Temple, dedicated to Hathor, goddess of love, music and the dance, and to Ramses' favorite queen, Nefertari.

Stonecutters chiseled the facade into the mountainside, imitating the stone pylons of Karnak and other temples. Then they fashioned four, 67-foot-high statues of a seated Ramses on the facade; Nefertari's tomb was granted only two statues, a mere 33 feet high, each flanked by two statues of Ramses.

Engineers from the City of the Dead at Thebes drilled tunnels into the rock, hollowing out a temple in the cliff as though it were in the open, and leaving rock pillars in place for support. In the Great Hall of Ramses' temple, craftsmen transformed pillars into statues holding the crook and flail, symbols common to both Ramses and the god Osiris. In the inner sanctum, craftsmen carved four seated figures out of the rock, representing Ramses and the gods Ptah, Amun and Re-Harakhti.

The two temples were completed before the 34th year of Ramses' reign, but some archeologists believe that while the pharaoh was still alive the second colossus on the south side of the facade fell to the sands, where it lay through the centuries. The architects had underestimated the fissures and stresses in the rock. Priests maintained the shrines for a while after Ramses' death. But by 1000 B.C., Lower Nubia had begun to fade from the pages of history, and the desert sands of the slowly reclaimed the Great Temple.

In the sixth century B.C., Greek and Phoenician mercenaries marching against Nubia climbed the sand dunes smothering the statues and carved some graffiti across Ramses' shin. The Small Temple, though, remained uncovered, and served as a refuge from marauding nomads.

The Great Temple slumbered undisturbed until 1813, when British adventurer John Lewis Burckhardt saw "what is yet visible of four immense colossal statues." He saw only the double crown, head and part of the torso of the most southerly statue and the two "bonnets" of the two northerly ones. He couldn't even tell if the statues were seated or standing.

Giovanni Battista Belzoni, a six-foot, six-inch Italian explorer, journeyed to Abu Simbel in 1817, dug through the sand, and gained entrance to the Great Temple. He and his cohorts marveled at carvings, paintings and sculptures unseen since ancient times. The southernmost colossus was dug out in 1819 and the general sand level was lowered, setting off a rush of tourists to view the imposing site.

▲ *Abu Simbel: "A mansion...for the great royal wife Nefertari," proclaims a dedication in hieroglyphs on the facade of the Small Temple. This shrine and the nearby Great Temple of Ramses were reassembled on higher ground.*

In 1964-68, a modern engineering marvel matched the achievement of the ancient architects. Thirty-two centuries after its construction, Abu Simbel was threatened by the rising Nile waters backed up by the Aswan High Dam. A mammoth international campaign spearheaded by UNESCO raised funds to save the two shrines. The temples were cut into 1,050 pieces weighing up to 33 tons, and reassembled on higher ground, complete even to the surrounding cliffs. Engineers completed the job with just three months to spare—one of the most dramatic rescue missions in history.

The re-creation of the rock-hewn temples enabled engineers to install such modern amenities as electric lighting and ventilation systems. The restoration of the rock framing the temple facades changed the perspective of the site somewhat. The hills are 76 and 52 feet lower than the old cliffs. The enormous cost of restoration made an exact duplicate of the original site out of the question. All traces of the cutting were camouflaged; six miles of joints were filled so carefully that most visitors can no longer find them. On the cliff faces around the facades, another ten miles of joints were hidden.

▲ *Abu Simbel: "Carved to last for eternity" says an inscription on the Great Temple of Ramses II. These four colossal statues of the pharaoh dominate the facade; a statue of the hawk-headed god Re, guards the entrance.*

Nile. When Alexander got there, a flock of birds suddenly darkened the sky. Alexander took this portent to mean that he should erect the new capital on that spot. The city which was to bear his name became the premier center of learning in the ancient world, home of antiquity's greatest library, and site of the lighthouse that was one of the Seven Wonders of the Ancient World.

The building of Alexandria was to profoundly change the course of history, for it opened the ancient land of Egypt to the vigorous Mediterranean influences of Greece and Rome. It was also an act of arrogance to build a capital here: Alexander's prophetic birds blackened the sky at an unfortunate spot. It had a swampy shoreline, dangerous offshore currents, and pirate-infested marshes nearby.

Despite this inauspicious location, Alexander called in his best city planner, Dinocrates, and most skillful engineers to build two artificial ports. Since the site lacked fresh water, they constructed a three-tiered, square-vaulted system of subterranean cisterns, which formed an underground city.

Alexander soon departed for the East, and never lived to see his beautiful city. After his death in 323 B.C., his body was returned to Alexandria and buried in a magnificent mausoleum. The ceremony was described in great detail by Diodorus, but by the fourth century A.D., when St. John Chrysostom asked to see the tomb, no one knew its whereabouts.

Another treasure that has been lost is the famous library of Alexandria. At the time of Ptolemy Philadelphus' death in 246 B.C., it housed more than 400,000 books. It was damaged by fire in 48 B.C., when Caesar invaded the city, and was finally burned to the ground in 391 A.D. Curiously, the Muslim population claimed responsibility for the destruction of the library; they considered books "useless if they confirm the Koran, harmful if they contradict it."

The destruction of Alexandria's library has been described as one of the most unfortunate events in the history of mankind. It was the "memory of the world," part of the Museum of Alexandria founded by Ptolemy Philadelphus. This lavishly endowed center of learning attracted the age's outstanding scientists, philosophers and men of letters, including mathematicians like Euclid, who wrote *Elements* in Alexandria, geographers like Eratosthenes, who calculated the size of the earth to within a few hundred miles, early physicians like Herophilus and Erasistratus, and the botanist Theophrastus.

The city declined even before the establishment of the capital at Cairo in the tenth century. The renowned lighthouse, 500 feet in height and the world's tallest building in its time, survived with numerous repairs from 280 B.C. until the 14th century, when it was toppled by an earthquake. Alexandria began a revival in the early 1800s under Muhammed Ali, founder of modern Egypt. It played a major role during World War II, an era described in romantic terms by Lawrence Durrell in his *Alexandria Quartet*: "A city at once sacred and profane."

Today, the city of four million is the country's major port, and a modern city that seems slightly rundown. Little remains to recall the glory of its Ptolemaic period. There is Pompey's Pillar, a 90-foot column that was actually dedicated to the Roman emperor Diocletian, and the remains of the nearby Temple of Serapis, dedicated to a god who manifested himself in the form of a bull.

Far to the east, near the foot of brooding Mount Sinai, stands the Monastery of St. Catherine, built on the traditional site where God spoke to Moses from the burning bush, commanding him to de-

Alexander and St. Catherine

E gypt wore the yoke of Persian domination for 200 years after the last pharaoh of the Twenty-ninth Dynasty was defeated in 525 B.C. at Pelusium, near today's Tell al-Faramah, east of the Suez Canal. After Alexander the Great defeated the Persians in 332 B.C., he liberated Egypt and appointed Ptolemy Soter, one of his Macedonian generals, as satrap (governor). Ptolemy founded the Ptolemaic dynasty, which ruled Egypt for 300 years until its conquest by the Romans in 30 B.C.

According to Plutarch, after Alexander visited the oracle of Amun at Siwa Oasis, near Egypt's present-day border with Libya, the great general had a dream commanding him to go to Pharos Island at the mouth of the western branch of the

▲ *Near Aswan: The Temple of Philae, including this section called the Kios of Trajan, was partially submerged after the first Aswan Dam was constructed at the turn of the century. The temple has been moved to a higher site.*

▲ *Edfu: The sky god Horus, represented as a falcon, guards the entrance to his temple at a spot halfway between Luxor and Aswan.*

► *Kom Ombo: The temple here was built about 200 B.C. by Ptolemy V and dedicated to two deities: Sobek and Horus. Thus most of its elements are double, like the dual doorways leading from the vestibule to the hypostyle hall.*

liver the children of Israel out of the land of Egypt. Later, on Sinai's summit, Moses received the Ten Commandments: "tables of stone, written in the finger of God."

The Byzantine Emperor Justinian the Great erected the monastery as a combination fortress and shrine. It still stands, after 1,400 turbulent years—one of the oldest active monasteries in existence, and an astounding repository of ancient manuscripts and works of art.

About the size of a city block, the monastery lies against one slope of a steep-sided wadi, girdled by a granite wall 12 to 15 feet thick and pierced by only one door. Inside is a miniature town with narrow paved streets, small courts, covered passages and whitewashed buildings piled on top one another—a glimpse of the vanished world of Byzantium.

The monastery library contains an extraordinary collection of some 3,000 ancient manuscripts—making this the world's richest monastic library. Texts in Greek, Arabic, Syriac, Georgian, Slavonic, Ethiopic and other languages span more than 1,500 years of Christianity.

The most valuable volume in the library was checked out in 1844 by a German scholar named Konstantin von Tischendorf, and never returned. The priceless book is the rare fourth-century *Codex Sinaiticus,* one of the three oldest extant manuscripts of the Bible. Tischendorf recognized its value and took it to Russia, where it remained until purchased by the British Museum in 1933. Tischendorf claimed he bought the *Codex* honestly from the monks, but in a letter written by the scholar in Greek and dated Sep-

tember, 1859, Tischendorf promises to return the volume to the monastery after completing his study of it. The original letter and an English translation now hang on the library wall.

The monastery church is the original structure, built between 548 and 565. Except for Hagia Sophia in Istanbul, it is the best-preserved survivor of the countless churches erected by Justinian. A marble tomb in the church contains the remains of the monastery's patroness, St. Catherine of Alexandria. Jeweled reliquaries contain the hand and skull of the fourth-century martyr, who was executed for chastising Emperor Maximinus for his persecution of Christians. After she was tortured on the wheel and beheaded, the story goes, angels carried her body to Mount Sinai.

Behind the apse is the Chapel of the Burning Bush. A simple marble slab surmounted by an altar marks the traditional spot where God commissioned Moses to deliver the children of Israel out of Egypt. Red vigil candles flicker eternally, recalling the bush which "burned with fire, and . . . was not consumed."

The monastery contains some of Christendom's most beautiful and rarest

▲ The salty waters of the Red Sea lap the barren sands of the Arabian peninsula.

◄ Although the ancient Egyptians only knew how to make linen by the fourth century A.D., some craftsmen along the Nile had begun to add colorful embroidered wool borders to the fabric.

mosaics and icons (perhaps 2,000 in all). Their existence is due, in part, to Islam. When Muslims conquered this region, the monastery became a Christian island severed from Byzantium. Later, at the time of the iconoclasts during the eighth century, the Byzantine emperors in Constantinople ordered all holy images destroyed, on the grounds that their use in Church rites constituted idolatry. But St.

Catherine's monks, isolated from mainstream Christianity, ignored the edict. Thus, the Sinai outpost is one of the very few surviving respositories of figure mosaics from the period.

The most splendid work is the great Transfiguration mosaic that arcs above the altar of the monastery church. Though slightly larger than life-size, the figures of Christ, Elijah the prophet, Moses and the

others seem monumental. The monastery's early icons show a technique similar to that employed by painters of Egyptian mummy portraits.

Perhaps the monastery's most beautiful icon is a seventh-century portrait of St. Peter clutching the keys to the kingdom of heaven in one hand, and his cross in the other. His penetrating gaze focuses sharply on eternity in this masterpiece.

▲ *Sinai Peninsula: Oasis of faith on the legendary site of the burning bush, St. Catherine's Monastery was founded by the Roman emperor Justinian. It houses a priceless collection of icons and manuscripts.*

► *Elephantine Island, Aswan: Verdant contrast to the sere slopes on the far bank of the Nile, this island has a profusion of gardens and palm trees, making it a cool and enchanting place to visit.*

107

Minarets and Highrises

Cairo is a relatively young city. It grew up in the shadow of the pyramids of Giza, which were already 3,500 years old when the new capital was founded in A.D. 969.

Legend has it that on an August day of that year, a conquering general named Jawhar commanded his soldiers to rope off a site northeast of what was then the capital of Egypt, El Fustat. The ropes formed a square about 1,200 yards on each side, and attached to them were many bells. At the moment when astrologers determined the planets were aligned properly in the sky, the bells would be rung and construction would begin on this new seat of government.

Unfortunately, a raven (perhaps a descendant of the flock that darkened the sky for Alexander) landed on the ropes, setting off the bells. The workmen dutifully began turning over the earth with their shovels. The bird's timing was bad—the planet Mars was rising, which the astrologers believed to be an ill omen. It was too late to turn back, so the astrolo-

gers decided to appease the fates by naming the city El Qahira (The Victorious) after El Qahir (Mars). The name was anglicized to Cairo.

The astrologers' trick seems to have worked, although the city's location at the junction of Lower and Upper Egypt—the delta and the valley—didn't hurt. The Nile was nearby, less than a mile to the west of the original site. To the east were the sheltering Muqattam Hills and enough pastures to graze goats and lambs, and feed a city.

Today, a population of ten million people makes Cairo the largest city in Africa and one of the world's most crowded urban areas. Cairo struggles to make room for a thousand newcomers each day, most refugees from the poverty of village life. In some ways, Cairo itself is just one enormous village, where extended families live together (sometimes crowding nine to a room) and where livestock is still kept.

The streets are as safe at night as those of a small town in Upper Egypt; there are few thieves and violence is almost unknown. Traffic accidents are the only real danger in Cairo: bus crashes can cause great loss of life because the vehicles are so crowded that many passengers hitch rides by standing on bumpers and clinging stubbornly to windows.

Despite the overcrowding, Cairenes maintain their cheerfulness and hospitality. At Sham ennessim, the feast of spring, the inhabitants of the poorer districts invade the smallest strip of garden or lawn to unpack a picnic consisting of *foul* (bean stew), *fessikh* (marinated fish) and sweets.

Cairo wears many faces. There is Islamic Cairo, with its narrow alleys and covered passageways. There is a European Cairo, there is a Cairo straight out of the Arabian nights, and there is a modern Arab Cairo, where tall apartment blocks flank broad boulevards.

One of the most fascinating neighborhoods is on the site of El Fustat. This is the location of the Roman-Byzantine Fortress of Babylon, which was besieged by a general of the Caliph of Bagdad in A.D. 640. According to legend, two doves had nested on the general's tent and, not wishing to disturb them, he left the tent in place after he conquered the Fortress of Babylon and continued his march to

Alexandria. The tent became the center of a garrison town which the soldiers dubbed El Fustat (The Tent).

Christians were permitted to practice their religion and build churches and monasteries there and today this walled quarter is still the heart of the Coptic world. Passing between two bastions from the Fortress of Babylon, visitors enter the peaceful oasis of the Coptic

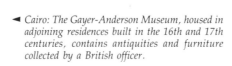

◄ *Cairo: The Gayer-Anderson Museum, housed in adjoining residences built in the 16th and 17th centuries, contains antiquities and furniture collected by a British officer.*

Museum. Many of the objects and paintings here have been preserved by the dry climate of Egypt, particularly the frescoes of Egypt's two most important Coptic monasteries, Bawit and Saqqara. Daniel's lion, wide-eyed and Cupidlike figures called Ledas, flights of ibis, graceful gazelles—all retain their fresh color.

The museum clearly illustrates the two influences of Coptic art. One is a form of Grecian art—profane, clever and sensual. The other is a popular form of naive and vigorous Christian art, which lasted into the 14th and 15th centuries, well after the conquest of Islam.

Coptic art received its best-known expression in textiles, displayed prominently in the museum. Pharaonic Egypt knew how to make plain linens, which were then painted or embroidered. The Copts invented new ways of weaving materials into geometrical patterns or designs with plants and figures.

The museum also reveals the art of Coptic wood-carvers, who fashioned lecterns, pilgrims' litters, altars, chairs inlaid with mother-of-pearl and ivory, and iconostases (screens), from the tenth-century Church of St. Barbara. The most impressive carved items display the art of

▲ *Cairo: Behind the central fountain and arched cloisters of the Mosque of Ibn Tulun rise the red ramparts of the Citadel of Saladin, capped by the slender minarets and alabaster domes of the Mohammed Ali Mosque.*

111

dates from the 13th century. It was used for performing a washing ritual required of Muslims before prayer. The minaret offers an excellent view of the Citadel and the Old City.

The Mamluks, who were emancipated Turkish slaves brought to Egypt as mercenaries by the Fatimites, endowed Cairo with many monuments after they began to rule in 1250. Their mosques, *madrasas* (Koranic schools) and mausoleums borrowed elements from Anatolia, Syria and Mesopotamia, but nevertheless managed to create a pleasingly homogeneous and original style all their own. Prayer halls were roofed with cupolas, and doors were high, unlike those of Turkish and Persian mosques.

But above all, Mamluk designs in Cairo broke the bonds of Islamic symmetry in a spectacular manner. Doorways are at the end of a facade and sometimes set back; a single minaret is seemingly positioned at random. When two minarets were used in a mosque, the classical tradition of balance was rejected in favor of an asymmetrical arrangement.

This aesthetic feat is perfectly achieved in an extraordinary monument, the Tomb Mosque of Sultan Barkuk. It is the finest mausoleum in the City of the Dead, a complex of two cemeteries in the southeast corner of Cairo. One cemetery contains the Tombs of the Caliphs and the other, called the Southern Necropolis, contains homes built by wealthy families for their dead relatives. At certain times of the year, the living would visit the cemetery to spend a few days with the dearly departed. The solitude and agonizing beauty at dusk make this one of the most compelling places in Cairo.

Many consider the Mosque of Sultan Hassan to be the most important Mamluk legacy in Cairo. Dating from the 1350s, it was built on a vast scale, appropriate to the land of the pyramids. It contains not only a mosque, but also a *madrasa*—a sort of boarding school for all four of the Islamic schools of law. Surprisingly, the artistic treasures in this structure are on a small scale: the white marble plaques carved with clusters of peonies and chrysanthemums; the shimmering stalactite dome; the stucco inscriptions.

The Mamluks ruled Egypt for 267 years. In 1517, Ottoman Turks stormed into the country, hanged the last Mamluk sultan and nailed his body to one of the massive gates in the city wall. The Ottomans governed Egypt as a province of their empire for 300 years.

moucharabieh—the delicate carving of screened balconies. These wood carvings are full of flights of fancy: pagan deities wandering by the Nile, papyrus thickets opening to reveal the jaws of a crocodile, and flocks of ibis.

Although the Christian community remained vigorous, the ascendancy of Islam after the tenth century turned Cairo into the "city of a thousand minarets." None rivals the Mosque of el Azhar as a physical and spiritual center of the medieval walled city of Cairo. Begun in 969 as the congregational mosque for the newly founded city, it became a leading Islamic center of learning, and is considered the oldest continuously operated university in the world.

The oldest mosque in Cairo is the Mosque of Ibn Tulun, built by Ahmad Ibn Tulun during the ninth century in the style of the great mosque of Samarra in Iraq. It has a simple, austere beauty that sets it apart from the more ornate styles of later centuries. The arcade has well-preserved examples of delicate arabesque designs in stucco under the arches. The pavilion in the center of the courtyard

▲ *Cairo: The ninth-century Mosque of Ibn Tulun combines such diverse architectural influences as an outside spiral staircase reminiscent of Samarra in Iraq and a Moorish belltower.*

Construction on a grand scale resumed under the reign of Mohammed Ali. He built the Mohammed Ali Mosque as part of the Citadel of Cairo, which was started in the 12th century by Saladin. Known as the Alabaster Mosque, this 19th-century baroque extravaganza is thoroughly Turkish. It is surrounded by a colonnade topped by small domes in a Turkish style; the small domes in turn are capped by the mosque's large central dome. At the back of the structure is a small garden with breathtaking views of the city from its highest point.

In the center of the courtyard is a Turkish kiosk which now serves as an ablution fountain. Also in the courtyard is a French baroque clock, which King Louis-Philippe of France swapped with Mohammed Ali for the obelisk that now stands in the Place de la Concorde in Paris. The French got the best of the deal—the obelisk is still standing but the clock has never worked.

The dynasty founded by Mohammed Ali continued until 1952, at least technically. Late in the 19th century, Britain took over the affairs of the bankrupt nation, occupied the capital, and created a constitutional monarchy. This neo-colonial state of affairs lasted until Colonel Gamal Abdel Nasser overthrew King Farouk in 1952. For the first time since before the birth of Christ, Egyptians took control of their own country.

For a taste of medieval Cairo, visitors throng the Khan et Khalili bazaar, originally laid out in the 15th century. Some 12,000 shops line the narrow streets, selling everything from samovars to spices. The bazaar is informally divided into sections that specialize in certain goods—gold, perfumes and cosmetics, jewelry, pottery, cloth, even pickles.

A merchant named Garkas el-Khalili started the bazaar about 1430. He saw a need for a central market, as well as a place where foreign merchants could live while in town to sell their goods. Today, many of these *wikalas,* or plots, have been transformed into artists' ateliers, some of which can be visited. In others, apprentices still learn the age-old trades of their ancestors.

▲ Cairo: At the foot of the Citadel, before the crenellated towers of Bab el-Azab, happy crowds throng to celebrate Cham en-Nesseim (Feast of Spring) on Salah ed-Din Square.

▲ Cairo: This colorful street scene is from the partially walled neighborhood of Old Cairo. It was originally the site of a Roman encampment called the Fortress of Babylon.

But the highlight of any visit to Cairo is the Egyptian Museum, that extraordinary attic of antiquity. It holds thousands of masterpieces, organized in roughly chronological order. Some of the best items from the Old and Middle kingdoms include a statue of the nobles Rahotep and Nofret, another of the dwarf Seneb and his wife and family, and a frieze known as "the Meidum Geese."

Treasures from the New Kingdom include pieces from Tell el Amarna—the city of the heretic king, Akhenaten, and his beautiful wife, Nefertiti. The pride of the museum is the treasure from the tomb of Tutankhamun, including the glorious golden death mask.

This wondrous collection also includes an exhibit of mummified sacred animals from various ancient Egyptian cults, including baboons, fish, crocodiles, dogs and cats. Another celebrated artifact is the Palette of Narmer. This 25-inch slate carving shows the Emperor Narmer, or Menes, in the crown of Upper Egypt about to strike an enemy from the Delta. Narmer forged the two Egypts into one, forever united by the Nile.

▲ *Dendereh: The primitive frescoes that adorn this dwelling illustrate the pilgrimage the Muslim owner made to Mecca.*

▲ *Near Dendereh: This timeless scene of white-turbanned fellahins driving their flocks beneath the ancient palms conjures up images of eternal, changeless Egypt.*

LANDS OF THE NILE: A Visitor's Guide

The lands of the Nile embrace a wide diversity of cultures and political systems, from the tribes of Tanzania and Uganda in "black" Africa to the Muslim countries of Egypt and Sudan, from the Marxist regime in Ethiopia to the shaky democracy of Kenya.

This part of Africa has been ravaged in recent years by civil wars, drought and famine, making travel there difficult in some cases and unthinkable in others. Despite these serious problems, tourism to this volatile part of the world has been increasing, for the area has so much to offer. The magnificent wildlife of East Africa, the ancient monuments of Egypt, the medieval churches of Ethiopia, the spice island of Zanzibar . . . all these destinations attract travelers in search of exotic adventure. Africa of the Nile offers it in abundance.

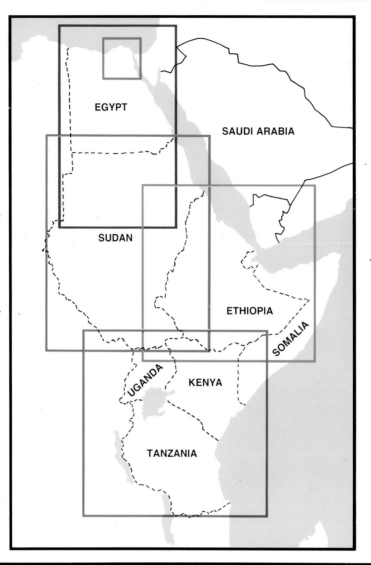

■ *KENYA, UGANDA, TANZANIA*
■ *ETHIOPIA*
■ *SUDAN*
■ *EGYPT*
■ *EGYPT (DETAIL)*

TOURING KENYA

How to get there

The international airports at Nairobi and Mombasa are served by several major airlines, including KLM, British Airways, TWA, Pan Am and Swissair. By far the cheapest alternative is to join a pre-packaged tour with the airfare included.

All travelers must have a valid passport and a valid round-trip or onward ticket. American travelers also require a visa, which costs $10. Visitors from Commonwealth countries (except Australia) do not need visas.

Currency

The unit of currency is the Kenya shilling, divided into 100 cents. Twenty shillings equal one Kenyan pound.

Foreign currency brought into Kenya must be declared upon entry. A record must be kept of all foreign currency exchanged during a visit; this may be required on departure. Kenyan currency cannot be taken out of the country.

Medical services

Kenya has a generally healthy climate. Tap water in cities is safe. Swimming is popular in the ocean, but should be avoided in rivers and lakes due to widespread bilharzia. Kenya requires no specific inoculations, but suggests visitors take an antimalarial drug.

There are public and private hospitals in Nairobi and Mombasa, but elsewhere health facilities are limited.

For a modest fee, travelers can buy a temporary membership in the East African Flying Doctor Services, P.O. Box 30125, Nairobi. Any member who becomes injured or ill while on safari in East Africa can receive free air transport to a medical center.

Climate

Kenya is an equatorial country, but its average altitude of 4,000 feet makes for a comfortable climate. The average temperature in Nairobi is 66°F in March and 61°F in July. The coastal climate is tropical and hot. Average temperatures in Mombasa are 80°F in March and 75°F in July.

The rainiest season is April and May.

The hottest months are February and March, the coolest June and July. The best time to visit Kenya is between December and April, during the dry, sunny season.

Language

Swahili is Kenya's lingua franca; however, English is widely spoken, even in many remote bush villages.

Getting around

Kenya has two international airports, Jomo Kenyatta in Nairobi and Moi at Mobasa. Kenya Airways operates an extensive internal service, including scheduled flights to Mombasa, Malindi and Kisumu.

Kenya Railways Corporation runs passenger trains between Nairobi and Mombasa, with regular connections to Kisumu and Malaba, and along branch lines to Nyeri and Nanyuki.

All major roads are now paved but vast areas of the north have little means of communication. Kenya is well-served by long-distance taxis which carry up to seven passengers. The most efficient of these services link Nairobi with Nakuru and Mombasa.

For more information

Kenya Tourist Office, 60 East 56th Street, New York, NY 10022

Kenya Tourist Office, 9100 Wilshire Boulevard, Doheny Plaza, Suite 111, Beverly Hills, CA 90121

Kenya High Commission, Gillin Building, Suite 600, 141 Laurier Avenue, Ottawa, Ontario K1P 5J3

TOURING UGANDA

How to get there

Entebbe Airport is serviced by British Airways, Sabena, Kenya Airways, Air Tanzania, Ethiopian Airlines, Air Zaire, Uganda Airlines and Aeroflot.

All travelers must have a valid passport, a round-trip or onward ticket, and a visitor's pass from the Uganda Tourism Development Corporation, P.O. Box 7211, Kampala, Uganda. American travelers must also obtain a visa from a Ugandan mission abroad.

Currency

The unit is the Uganda shilling. Coins are in denominations of one shilling, 50 cents and five cents. Denominations of currency are in notes of five, 10, 20, 50, 100, 500, and 1,000 shillings.

Medical services

All visitors are required to show an international certificate of vaccination against yellow fever and cholera. Most parts of Uganda are free from malaria, but inoculation is recommended to reduce risk. Tap water is usually not safe to drink, even in the cities. Bilharzia contaminates most lakes, except Lake Nabugabo and Lake Bunyonyi. Medical facilities are not well developed.

Climate

Uganda straddles the equator, but the climate is pleasant due to the low humidity and high altitude. Temperatures seldom rise above 85°F or fall below 65°F. An annual average rainfall of 380 inches keeps the countryside green year-round. Rain falls heavily in March-May and October-November.

Language

English is the official language. Swahili is the national language, and numerous local dialects are also spoken.

Getting around

Uganda Airlines provides service between the airport at Entebbe, (southeast of the capital) and Arua, Gulu, Masindi, Pakuba, Kasese and Mbarara. Upon final departure from the country, a tax of 3,000 shillings is charged at Entebbe.

A rail network links most parts of the country, and all the main towns are connected by paved roads. Visitors requiring chauffeur-driven cars are advised to book through their travel agents before arrival. All visitors in possession of a valid driving license are permitted to drive in Uganda.

For more information

Uganda Embassy, 5909 16th St. NW, Washington, D.C. 20011

Uganda High Commission, 170, Laurier Avenue, Suite 601, Ottawa, Ontario K1P 5V5

TOURING TANZANIA

How to get there

Tanzania is served by several international airlines, including British Airways, Air France, Alitalia, EgyptAir, KLM, Lufthansa, SAS, Sabena and Swissair. International airports are at Dar es Salaam and Kilimanjaro.

Commonwealth visitors do not require a visa. American travelers require a visa, obtainable from the Tanzania Embassy.

Currency

The unit of currency is the Tanzanian shilling, divided into 100 cents.

Tanzania enforces its strict exchange control laws. Foreign currency brought into Tanzania must be declared upon entry. A record must be kept of all foreign currency exchanged during a visit, and produced upon departure. Traveler's cheques may be cashed only at authorized

dealers (banks, hotels). When leaving, travelers may not take more than 100 shillings out of Tanzania.

Medical services

Malaria is prevalent, except at altitudes over 5,000 feet. Although inoculation is not required, it is recommended that visitors begin taking antimalarial pills two weeks before arrival and for two weeks after departure.

The water in all urban and tourist areas is chemically treated and safe. It is advised, though, to bring medication in case of dysentery.

All urban areas have modern hospitals, and many rural areas are served by clinics. Tanzania is also served by the East African Flying Doctor Services (see Kenya). For further information, contact the East African Flying Doctor Services, Kilimanjaro Christian Center, P.O. Box 3010, Moshi, Tanzania.

Climate

Tanzania is a tropical country, but its climate is determined by altitude. The most pleasant weather along the coast is found from June to September. The best seasons for photography safaris are November to March and June to October

in northern Tanzania; June to November in southern, central and western Tanzania; and July to November for the Selous and Rungwa reserves.

Language

Swahili is the national language, although local dialects prevail; English is widely spoken throughout the country.

Getting around

Air Tanzania, launched in 1977, serves all main towns. The national parks have air strips, and charter companies based in Dar es Salaam fly single- and twin-engine aircraft to numerous bush strips in remote parts of the country.

Most major towns are on the rail network operated by Tanzania Railways, and Tanzania has a good network of paved roads connecting major centers (traffic drives on the left). An international driving license is required. Renting a car, though, is extremely expensive.

For more information

Tanzania Embassy, 2139 R St. NW, Washington, D.C. 2008

Tanzania High Commission, 50 Range Road, Ottawa, Ontario K1N 8J4

TOURING ETHIOPIA

How to get there

Ethiopian Air flies to Addis Ababa from Athens, Frankfurt, London, Paris, Rome and other major centers. The country is also served by British Airways, Air France, Alitalia, Lufthansa and other carriers.

Visitors holding valid passports can obtain 30-day tourist visas on arrival at the international airports at Addis Ababa and Asmara. Tourist visas for up to three months can be obtained from Ethiopian missions abroad.

Currency

The unit of local currency is the Ethiopian *birr*. Foreign currency must be declared on entry. Money can be exchanged only at the National Bank of Ethiopia, but traveler's cheques can be cashed at banks and hotels.

Medical services

Vaccination against yellow fever is required, and vaccination against typhus, typhoid and tetanus is recommended.

KENYA, UGANDA, TANZANIA

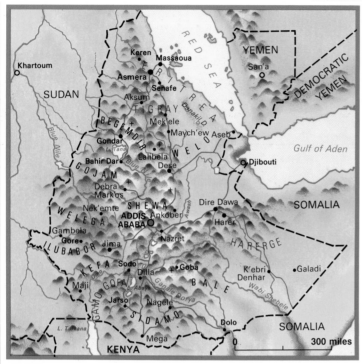

Antimalarial medication should also be taken before arrival.

Drink only boiled or bottled water. Avoid swimming in rivers and lakes due to widespread bilharzia. The country's hot springs and the alkaline lakes of Debre Zeyt and Langano are safe for swimming.

Climate

Ethiopia's coastal regions and the Denakil plains are among the hottest places in the world. But on the central plateau, where the capital and most of the historic sites are located, the climate is a pleasant 50°F to 75°F throughout the year. The "big rains" which account for most of the country's precipitation usually occur from mid-June to September. The current devastating drought proves that this is not always the case.

Language

Ethiopia's official language, Amharic, is spoken through the country, and the knowledge of a few simple phrases will help the visitor feel at home. English is the second official language, and understood in the larger towns. French, Italian and Arabic are also widely spoken.

Getting around

The most convenient—and sometimes the only—way to get around is by air. Ethiopian Airlines operates flights to some 40 towns throughout the country.

All-weather roads now link the provincial capitals and major tourist areas (driving is on the right). For stays of more than a month, a temporary Ethiopian driving license will be issued upon presentation of a valid license from your home country. For stays of less than 30 days, use of the local license is permitted. A reliable and inexpensive bus system operates throughout the country.

For more information

Ethiopian Embassy, 2134 Kalorama Road NW, Washington, D.C. 20008 (For both U.S. and Canada)

TOURING SUDAN

How to get there

Khartoum is served by Air France, British Airways, Alitalia, KLM, Lufthansa, SAS, Swissair and many Middle Eastern carriers. The national airline, Sudan Airways, has flights from Egypt, Germany, Greece, Jordan, Italy, the UK and several other countries.

Arriving from Egypt could include the follow itinerary: by rail from Cairo to the Aswan High Dam, by steamer to Wadi Halfa, and by train to Khartoum.

All travelers must have a passport valid for at three months beyond the length of their intended stay, and a visa, which should be obtained in advance from a Sudanese mission abroad. Visas are not issued at the airport. Admission to Sudan is refused to holders of Israeli passports, or passports with an expired or valid visa for Israel or South Africa.

A special permit is required to visit the southern Sudan. It can be obtained from a mission abroad or from the Ministry of the Interior at Khartoum.

Currency

The monetary unit is the Sudanese pound, which is divided into 100 piastres (PT) or 1,000 millimes.

Foreign currency, including traveler's cheques, cash and letters of credit, must be declared on entry and departure. Exchange should be made only at authorized outlets—banks, specified hotels and travel agencies—and entered on the declaration form which must be shown on departure.

Medical services

Inoculation against yellow fever and cholera is recommended; against malaria is also advisable, especially if traveling in the bush. The water supplies of major towns are safe to drink. Swimming is popular in the sea, but should be avoided in rivers and lakes due to widespread bilharzia.

Climate

The best time to visit Sudan is in winter—from November to March. Winter temperatures are about 60°F in the north and 80°F in the south. January is the coolest month in Khartoum. Summers are hot throughout the country, with temperatures ranging from 80° to 115°F.

Language

The official language of Sudan is Arabic, but English is widely spoken.

Getting around

Official permits are required for most journeys in Sudan; they can be obtained from the Registry Office in Khartoum. It is also advised to register with police in each town where you stay the night.

Sudan Airways' domestic service is subject to frequent and unpredictable change. Check your reservations and flight times until the moment of departure.

Sudan has the longest railway network in Africa. The trains are comfortable and clean in first class, but extremely slow. Major lines connect the capital with Port Sudan on the Red Sea, Wadi Halfa, El-Obeid, Nyala, Wau, Roseires and Kassala.

Sudan has very few paved roads. Although major work is being done to modernize the system, this method of transportation is not generally recommended. Motorists should inquire about road conditions and administrative restrictions in advance. Roads in the north are usually closed during the rainy season, from July to September.

Several Nile steamer excursions are suitable for tourists. The Dongola-Karima voyage takes two days. Service to the south is designed more for cargo and local travel than sightseeing.

For more information

Sudan Embassy, 2210 Massachussetts Ave. NW, Washington, D.C. 20008

Sudan Embassy, 457 Laurier Avenue, Ottawa, Ontario K1N 6R4

TOURING EGYPT

How to get there

Cairo's international airport is served by more than 20 international carriers, from Pan Am to EgyptAir.

All travelers must have a valid passport and a visa. If you fly to Cairo, visas are available upon entry but you may be asked to exchange the equivalent of $150 (US) into Egyptian pounds on the spot. This requirement is sometimes waived for travelers arriving with visas.

All visitors must register within a week of entering Egypt. Most hotels will send somebody to the Mugamma Building in Tahrir Square in Cairo with your passport, where it will be stamped.

Currency

The Egyptian pound is divided into 100 piastres (PT).

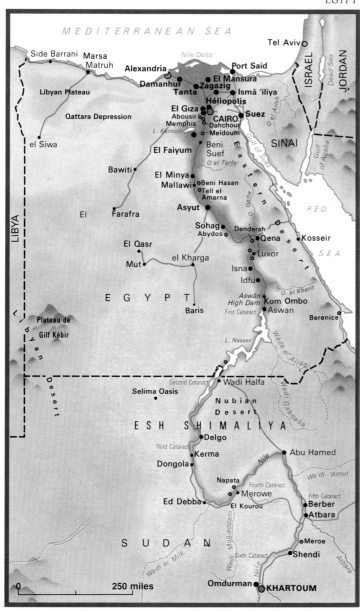

For more information

Write to an Egyptian consulate in the United States:

1110 Second Avenue, New York, NY 10022

505 North Shore Lake Drive, Suite 6502, Chicago, IL 60611

3001 Pacific Avenue, San Francisco, CA 94115

2310 Decatur Place NW, Washington, D.C. 20008

2000 West Loop South, Suite 1750, Houston, TX 77027

Egyptian Embassy, 454 Laurier Avenue, Ottawa, Ontario K1N 6R3

Egyptian Consulate, 3754 Cote des Neiges, Montreal, Quebec H3H 7V6

Dynasties of ancient Egypt

Early Dynastic Period (First to Third dynasties; c. 3100-2686 B.C.): The capital of Egypt is founded at Memphis by Menes.

Old Kingdom (Fourth to Sixth dynasties; c. 2686-2181 B.C.): The age of the pyramids and the sun god Re; the foundations of Egyptian art and architecture are laid by Zozer and his chief of works, Imhotep.

First Intermediate Period (Seventh to Tenth dynasties; c. 2181-2050 B.C.): Little-known period ends in civil war between rulers of Thebes and Heracleopolis.

Middle Kingdom (Eleventh and Twelfth dynasties; c. 2050-1786 B.C.): Upper and Lower Egypt are reunited under a series of powerful pharaohs such as Senusert III.

Second Intermediate Period (Thirteenth to Seventeenth dynasties; c. 1786-1567 B.C.): A series of weak rulers leads to a period of upheaval.

New Kingdom (Eighteenth to Twentieth dynasties; c. 1567-1085 B.C.): The Egyptian Empire reaches its zenith of power and influence in the ancient world under such

pharaohs as Hatshepshut, Amenhotep III, Akhenaten, Tutankhamun and Ramses II. Among the architectural treasures built during this period are the temple at Luxor, the Colossi of Memnon and the temples of Abydos and Abu Simbel.

Late Dynastic Period (Twenty-first to Thirtieth dynasties; 1085-332 B.C.): A period of general decline as Egypt becomes a virtual colony of Persia.

The Ptolemies (332-30 B.C.): Alexander the Great defeats the Persians and appoints Ptolemy Soter as governor. A new capital, Alexandria, is founded on the delta. Cleopatra tries unsuccessfully to preserve Egypt's independence.

Roman Period (30 B.C.-A.D. 337): Egyptian fields and quarries supply imperial granaries and roads. Christianity is introduced to Egypt, but the decline of Rome leads to religious persecution.

Byzantine Period (A.D. 337-642): Egypt falls prey to invaders from Nubia, Persia and west Africa. Monasticism grows in importance and endures through the centuries of Islamic rule that follow.

EGYPT (DETAIL)

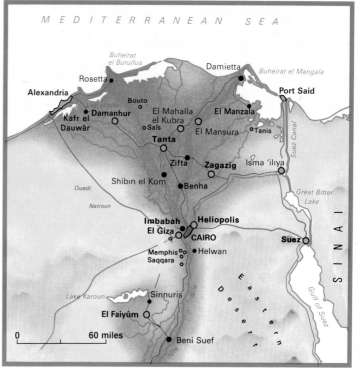

Foreign currency must be declared on entry. Visitors can bring in an unlimited amount of foreign currency and up to 20 Egyptian pounds. Egyptian pounds must be converted to a foreign currency before leaving the country.

Medical services

No inoculations are required, except for travelers arriving from Asia and Africa, and areas known to be infected with cholera and yellow fever.

Do not swim in the Nile; it is infected with bilharzia. To avoid upset stomach, do not eat fresh salads at less reputable restaurants and food stalls. Most major hotels have resident physicians who prescribe medication for minor ailments.

Climate

The best time to visit is during the winter, from October to April, when the average temperature is 62°F. This is also the main tourist season, however, when Egypt is most crowded. In summer, temperatures in Cairo can reach 110°F, and up to 125°F farther south, so there are fewer tourists

at the major sites. Alexandria becomes a crowded summer playground for tourists and Cairenes alike.

Language

Arabic is the official language; English and French are widely spoken, especially in tourist areas.

Getting around

EgyptAir operates daily flights from Cairo to the popular destinations of Luxor, Aswan, Abu Simbel, New Valley (Kharga Oasis) and Hurghada on the Red Sea.

Rail transportation is cheap, reasonably punctual and comfortable in air-conditioned first- and second-class cars. Third-class coaches can be extremely crowded. For first- and second-class seats, reserve at least a day in advance. Book several days in advance for sleeper compartments.

One of the most delightful ways to see the antiquities is by Nile steamer. Several cruise lines operate on the river, including the luxurious craft operated by the Sheraton and Hilton hotel chains.

PICTURE CREDITS

Credits are from left to right, top to bottom
with additional information if needed.

Cover: Daily Telegraph—Masterfile
2 Freeman Patterson—Masterfile; 3 Jeremy Ferguson—First Light
6-7 Jeremy Ferguson—First Light (2)
8 Jeremy Ferguson—First Light; Wayne Lynch—Masterfile
9 G. Gerster—Photo Researchers—Reflexion Photothèque
10 Jeremy Ferguson—First Light; 11 Denis Huot
12 C. Lénars; A. Robillard; 12-13 Langiaux—Fotogram
14 Durou—Jaffre: 15 Visage—Explorer
16 Denis—Fotogram; F. Varin; 16-17 Vulcain—Explorer
18 J. Bottin; 18-19 Rémy
20-21 J. Gabanou
22 M.-L. Maylin; 22-23 A. Hutchison Lby
24 Rémy; 24-25 A. Robillard
26 Vulcain—Explorer; 26-27 J. Bottin
28 Valentin—Explorer; 28-29 M. Pelletier
30 Enclebert-Rapho; 31 Tondeur—Atlas—Photo
32 Reichel—Top; 32-33 Gerster-Rapho
34 G. Annequin; 35 Gerster—Rapho
36 G. Annequin (2); 36-37 Dubois—Atlas—Photo
38 Froissardey—Atlas—Photo; J. Bottin; 39 G. Annequin
40 J. Bottin; 40-41 Gerster—Rapho
42-43 Gerster—Rapho (3)
44 G. Annequin; Cat—C.E.D.R.I.; 44-45 Gerster—Rapho
46 Froissardey—Atlas—Photo; 47 Minosa—Scorpio Films; Purcell—Rapho
47-48 G. Annequin (2)
50 J. Bottin; Gerster—Rapho; 51 G. Annequin
52 G. Annequin; 52-53 Gerster—Rapho
54 Minosa—Scorpio Films; 54-55 Gerster—Rapho
56-57 G. Annequin
58-59 Gerster—Rapho (2)
60 P. Challoy; Dubois—Atlas—Photo; 61 G. Annequin
62 Beuzen—Top; 63 Cat—C.E.D.R.I.
64 Hostal—Balafon; Rouilleaux—Sidoc; 64-65 Gerster—Rapho
66-67 Bernheim—Rapho (3)
68 Franceschi—Balafon; Brignolo—Image Bank
69 Hostal—Balafon; Dubois—Atlas—Photo
70-71 Bernheim—Rapho
72 Rouilleaux—Sidoc; 72-73 J. Bottin
74 Rouilleaux—Sidoc; 74-75 Rodger—Magnum
76 Rodger—Magnum; J. Bottin; 77 Rouilleaux—Sidoc
78 Garanger—Sipa—Press; 79 Beuzen—Top; C. Lénars
80 S. Held; 80-81 Sioen-C.E.D.R.I.; 81 S. Held
82-83 Ross—Rapho
84 Burnet—Contact; 85 Garanger—Sipa Press
86 P. Tétrel; 86-87 Sioen—C.E.D.R.I.
87-88 S. Held
90 Mathieu—A.F.I.P.; 91 Charbonnier—Top; J. Bottin
92 Charbonnier—Top; Marthelot—A.A.A. Photo; 92-93 S. Held
94 A. Gaël; (top) Villota—Image Bank; 94-95 Sioen—C.E.D.R.I.
96 C. Lénars; F. Daussint; 97 Georges—Sidoc
98 Frédéric—Rapho: P. Tétrel; 99 A. Gaël; S. Chirol
100 Launois—Rapho: Lessing—Magnum; 101 Brake—Rapho
102 F. Daussint; 102-103 P. Tétrel
104 P. Tétrel; S. Chirol; 105 Marthelot—A.A.A. Photo
106 P. Tétrel; Bright—Rapho; 106-107 Goldman—Rapho
108 Sioen—C.E.D.R.I.
110 Charbonnier—Top; 110-111 Gabanou—C.D. Tétrel
112 Chernush—Image Bank; 113 P. Tétrel (2)
114 S. Chirol; 114-115 Sioen—C.E.D.R.I.
Back cover: V. Englebert—Photo Researchers—Réflexion Photothèque